Unused

Towels

TABLE OF CONTENTS

My Thank You's

First, I thank God for loving me unconditionally and for guiding me to share these thoughts about my experiences using His God-loaned talents and skills, guiding me to leave this earth with as few unused talents and skills as possible.

Second, thank you to my Mary, who was honest most of the time as I began to write this book, choosing to prioritize "encouragement" in lieu of "edits," knowing that encouragement was more important than grammar in those early days.

I also thank her for always being there as I continued to write and struggle, when I needed her support, her patience, her guidance, her encouragement and her love.

Finally, I thank her for the very crucial role she has had in editing my final draft. Many of the pages that previously "hummed" now "sing" due to her priceless and inspired edits. Although the book is a collection of my experiences (with one exception), Mary's detailed editing has turned "my stories" into "our book." Thank you, Mary!

Third, thank you to Stephanie, although a stranger when we met in the line to get our Covid 19 vaccinations, she gave me crucially needed encouragement at just the right time when I was considering giving up writing this book. Thank you, Stephanie!

Fourth, thank you to Rose for being the quintessential expert at bringing my "draft" manuscript to this published work. Without Rose's assistance, I am not sure what my novice writer's fantasy would have accomplished. Thank you, Rose!

PREFACE - In Two and A Half Parts

This is not a traditional book; there is no main theme, character or plot. There are no main story-book elements. One need not read one chapter in order to have another chapter make sense; each chapter is a "stand-alone." It is a place to graze, a place to take a break, a place to sit back, relax and enjoy.

Consider the book "Readers-Digestesque," or, if one is fortunate enough to have experienced any of the J. Peterman Company owner's manuals, one could consider this book not unlike those manuals. For example, each of the 114 chapters in *Owner's Manual No. 8, Winter 1990* is a stand-alone chapter describing in glorious detail an item offered to be purchased after a fantasy-like discovery by Mr. J. Peterman. Again, there is no main theme, character or plot, just whimsical glowingly described *must-have* items: "The J. Peterman Coat. 'Classic horseman's duster protects you, your rump, your saddle and your legs down to the ankle. Because it's cut very long to do the job. It's unintentionally very flattering. With or without a horse. Although I live in horse country, I wear this coat for other reasons. Because they don't make Duesenbergs anymore.' J. Peterman."

Most of *Unused Towels* is a series of situations, some of which bring laughter, some of which evoke tears, some of which elicit deep thoughts, some of which are great for killing time while warming a cup of tea or coffee, "Oops, gotta go, the microwave just beeped."

These situations are included because at some point in my life as I was sharing these experiences, someone said, *Oh, that's a great story; you should write a book about that.*

So here it is.

Part Uno: Why I Am Writing This

I Do Not Wish To Die With Any "Unused Towels" In My Closet

When visiting my parents, I typically had to ask for at least two towels when preparing to take a shower; the towels provided by Mom or Dad were old and almost paper thin and if I wished to dry myself completely, two towels were necessary.

When I asked if they had any thicker towels there was a polite reply which belied the truth, "No."

There were in fact several new (thick) towels in the linen closet.

When I asked if I could use one, I was told lovingly that those towels were "for company."

With a smile, I tenderly replied, "But I **am** company."

Mom or Dad would calmly reply: "*No, you're not.* You're family."

Cutting my losses, I acquiesced with a barely audible, "Oh." (I did not wish to gamble on my also losing the toasted ends of Mom's perfectly baked meat loaf, her golden, yummy corn fritters, the completely moist *refritos,* and her distinctive, "Ooh, that smells so good" home-made bread ... maybe even home-made tortillas, with two "burnt" ones, one for her and one for me.)

The next time I visited I brought three sets of new towels, one for each of them and one "for family."

Not surprisingly, this did not help since the following time that I visited, none of the new towels were to be found. In addition, the linen closet where the towels had been stored now contained only pillow cases; no new towels were in sight.

I knew better than to ask where the new towels I had brought were. The only thing to do when next time I visited was to bring my own new towels and to take them with me when I left. (When Mom went to be with the Lord, Dad welcomed help from my sister and me to clean out the various closets where Mom's clothes were hanging or stored. With a smile, I found at least two dozen brand new, or barely used, towels in a corner of one of her closets. Without asking Pop, my sister took the thread-bare towels which were out "for family" to her home to use as rags. Pop seemed to be happy to have brand new towels with which to dry himself; no words were ever spoken about those towels. I suspected all along that this was "my little Polly's" decree. "You were a stinker, Mom!" That was only one of the many reasons why I loved her so much.)

So now one might say, "Cute," or, "Hmm, sort of interesting, but what does that have to do with anything that might be of interest to me?"

I offer this story because when the Good Lord takes me "home," I want to be sure that I have not left any *unused towels* hidden in any corners of "my God-given closet." I wish to assure that all of my talents were used to their fullest, that none of the skills that the Good Lord loaned me while on this earth were left unused.

Cleaning Out My Work Files

In cleaning out my forty-plus years of work files after five years of retirement, I found myself a bit sad, and also a bit proud. I had done some really good work. There were several truly exceptional results from the various training classes and other workshops for which I had been responsible. These conclusions were reinforced by people's complimentary feedbacks indicating a promise of continuing improvements in their own professional and personal lives.

This potential for improvements in their lives was likely stimulated by the fact that for most of the classes, I began by letting them know that my first experience as a manager/supervisor was a total disaster. I related how in less than three weeks I was able to bring the entire office with a staff of 13 persons to a complete halt by micro-managing the hell out of them.

Their reactions to this admission resulted in "knowing glances" at one another. After the laughter died down, I continued by letting them know that fortunately I was a fast learner.

I recounted how one Friday afternoon as people were filing out of the office, the person who believed that he should have been promoted to my position (Let's call him "Carl") stopped to let me know what a terrible job I was doing and how I was slowing everything down by my actions (basically consisting of an oft-repeated error of first-time managers, believing that I had to review and approve every bit of work being done in that office).

I told the class participants that fortunately the Good Lord had given me listening skills, which although I did not always use, Carl's words kicked in that Friday afternoon. I took to heart what he said to me. That weekend, I went into the office and cleared the stacks of work that I had in my "Review" in-box.

When the staff came in to work on Monday morning, they found *their* in-boxes full, with appropriate notes from me, all containing an apology from me.

After that, having learned to trust the staff, I began asking for their opinions. The result was that work previously taking two to four years to complete began being done in less than 15 months, the progress mostly due to the heightened level of mutual trust in the office and the resulting enriched pride in doing the work.

When the class participants' laughter had died down, their attention became more serious and attentive knowing that the lesson about how to become a better manager came to life in the stories of my real-life debacles and true lessons learned. Knowing that the classes were never simply about "book learning," folks responded in very positive ways. No time wasted in these classes or workshops! No *unused towels* left in those rooms!

I now find these accomplishments to be somewhat unbelievable since the timeframes for much of this work was many years ago. However, I do know that the great majority of the classes and workshops, along with the written materials, made life-lasting, positive changes in many lives: "Not only did you make my day, you helped me to change my life." "You've given me a new direction in my life." These types of comments were often repeated feedback.

A surprising majority of the persons in these workshops and classes continued to sign up for future classes. I sometimes had to schedule two or three days of the same class in order to accommodate their requests. Their keen attention during the classes, eyes fixated as well as their participation in the discussions reinforced the value of what God had passed on to me to pass on to them. I never had a problem getting volunteers to participate in scenarios which I created to bring the lesson points to life; participants were always quick to volunteer to be part of the case studies.

One set of handouts which I found in my files was for a workshop I conducted when one of my clients asked me if I could present an "Ethics in Government" workshop to his District managers and supervisors. Although this was a topic which I had never addressed in a class before, his agency was reeling from recent headline-news about the appearance of a few conflicts of interest. They were desperate and they trusted me enough to present relevant material, not a lecture but a "how to" discussion.

For some unknown reason, I kept my hand-written notes in addition to the printed materials from this specific workshop. In reading my notes, I was suddenly overcome with the depth of the material written and how well it was done. (Much of the credit for the extra depth of the material goes to my wife who was always essential in perfecting the bare skeleton of my basic thoughts and notes.)

As I read these workshop notes, I was surprisingly overcome with emotion to the point where tears were running freely down my face onto my chin. The preparation and materials were well done and were fully relevant to their circumstances. This had not been some theoretical class steeped in legal phrases; it was *real life* as they were experiencing it. (They subsequently requested the same class be repeated for several more groups in their organization.)

I am proud of that work and of their responses because they were evidence that my God-loaned talents were in fact being used. No *unused towels* there; the skills and talents were being passed on effectively! That makes me glad but also sad, sad that I no longer have a forum in which to continue to pass on all those God-loaned talents.

And so I write.

Would that I could write like Hugh Prather, *Notes To Myself, My Struggle To Become A Person*, first published by Real People Press in 1970 and later by Bantam Books. Would that I could write like Wm. Paul Young, author of *The Shack*, originally published by Windblown Media in 2007.

I mention *Notes To Myself* and *The Shack* since these are the only books which I have read multiple times; I am not one to re-read books. However, I have read *The Shack* as of today 11 times, cover to cover and am absolutely moved to make differences in my life and my relationship with God each time. Having bought *Notes To Myself* over 50 years ago, I have lost count of how many times I have read that treasure of thoughts and ideas from Mr. Prather.

[I have several copies of Hugh Prather's books, including two copies of *Notes To Myself*. One copy is autographed "Dear Fil, Walk in light, Love, Hugh, 1-14-99." Note: Mr. Prather went home to be with God on November 15, 2010.

I also found autographs from Gayle (Mrs. Prather), "Gayle, love," as an addendum to a second autograph from Hugh which reads, "To Fil and Mary. Treat each other gently, Hugh." What a delightful gift.]

Back to my God-loaned talents, I am proud that at one point in my life the work produced was absolutely excellent work! I nonetheless feel sad that the person about whom I am reading in these old work files (me) no longer exists in the same way that I *existed* when all this was taking place.

As I near my 80s, I am keenly aware of two things:

(1) The skills and talents which I shared with clients (including for-profit companies, several Boys & Girls Clubs, and a battered women's shelter), friends, family, and strangers over the last 40-plus years are as keen today as they were during my professional career; and

(2) I find myself doing what a lot of us at this stage in life seem to do more frequently, that is to offer advice (often unsolicited, or if solicited, more than what was requested) to anyone polite enough to seem to want to hear what I have to say. Fortunately, I am often reminded of what I used to think to myself about my Pop who, in his 80s and 90s, often seemed to believe that the femme fatales smiling with him were doing so because he was that sexy farm-boy stud that my mother had admired when she first saw him as a teenager, and not because he was a "cute old man." I remind myself, "He/she is listening to be polite, not necessarily because you are espousing words of wisdom, or, tales of entertainment, but because you have a nice head of white hair."

One of the Sunday cartoons I enjoy is *Agnes*, by Tony Cochran. In one cartoon, the two young girls are resting nostalgically against a bean bag.

Agnes says to her friend, "Sigh, all of our best years are behind us now."

Her friend replies, "No! I refuse! I have many more best years coming!"

To which Agnes replies, "No, honey. We've peaked. I think it was around spring of last year."

"No! I refuse peaking! I will not peak until I am old!"

"Ha! Who wants to peak when everything hurts and your nose dribbles in the cold?"

"Ok, fine. Maybe middle age ... Say twenty-two or three."

Oh, to be so young and naïve ... **and** full of confidence!

So Why Am I Writing This, Really?

Note: This section "So Why Am I Writing This, Really?" was written after several months of my writing "at this" near the end of the final draft. It is being inserted here because I asked my wife to help me talk myself into a decision as to whether I was serious about writing this book, or, deciding that it was merely a hobby. This was a very serious issue for me since I have had many bouts of not caring to write.

Fortunately, I was very perceptive in asking Mary for her assessment about these writings. She has a knack for "getting to the point" which I seem unwilling to do so often.

The result was a series of questions: *What is* my desired end goal? What are my desired objectives to reach that goal? What do I want people to get out of my book? When finished reading this book, what do I want them to say they got out of it? As they read this book, do I want them to laugh? Do I want them to cry? Do I want to touch their hearts? Do I want to touch their souls?

The answers were insightful: I wish to write a book that makes a difference in people's lives, a book that touches people's hearts, that touches people's souls, a book that helps people make a difference in how they see themselves, a book that helps them make a difference in how they go back into the world, a book that helps people not live in their failures but live in their successes, all this without preaching.

I am writing this to share my experiences, with some laughter, some tears, but with the hope that when people are finished reading it, it will have helped them forge a better relationship with themselves, where they will let "trust in God" control them, not letting anger or failures control them, where they will be buoyed by what is good in their own lives, in what and how they do things.

And so, I leave these thoughts so that should you wish to delve into them, it is with great joy that I share them with you. If you are merely being polite, then please feel free to go.

Nota Bene: I realized half-way into writing this book that what is most heart-felt in my thoughts relates to the pain of suicidal depression. Note that I am not talking about *suicide* but I **am** talking about suicidal depression.

I am reluctant to offer these thoughts since so much has been written about suicide. One would reasonably assume that there are enough experts out there, and therefore, I should likely question why what I have to offer could be of any value. However, most of what I have read is bull-caca.

What I offer are thoughts that I have not read anywhere else. This is especially true about my chapter titled "TOSTI," which includes thoughts that I have not found anywhere else. ("TOSTI" is my acronym for "The Other Side of The Ice," *an emotional state of mind where nothing matters; there is no such thing as love, help, caring, or any emotion.*)

That chapter may give some insight into the actions of a loved one prior to her/him *unexpectedly* taking their life. It may give understanding to someone who has wondered, "Where was the clue? How could I have missed the clue? I should have picked up on it. If only she/he had given me a clue." "Why didn't they tell me how they were feeling?" "I am so sorry that I missed the signs," or, "They seemed so happy; I don't understand why they took their life," or, "I never saw it coming; he/she was such a happy soul."

Trust me, having been prepared three times to *transition out of this life*, the moments before making that decision to take one's life is an empty place. It is a place that makes no sense.

It seems that I am deep-down writing this because of the many silently suffering from suicidal depression. If I can help even one person look into the eyes of someone suicidally depressed and help them bring that person back into the world on this side (the side where emotions exist), then I feel that I will not have left unused the most important towels in my God-loaned talents drawer.

If even only one person is helped, I thank God for having guided me to offer these words.

Part Dos:
This Is A Place To Graze;
It Is Neither A Novel Nor A Self-Help Book

Nineteen of the twenty-three chapters contain stories and experiences which are thought-provoking and have changed my life in very positive ways. When you feel the need for a break, these chapters are good options. Many of them are very short. Quite a few of them contain funny stories. Some invite *deep thinking*. Others require *no thinking*. ☺ Simply stated, these chapters are a place to graze.

There are four chapters which might produce some helpful insight to some readers: "I'm Sorry, Kids," "Living In My Failures," "Suicide," and "TOSTI."

"TOSTI" may be of special interest to anyone who may have wondered why someone took his or her own life when everything seemed to be going well.

All the other chapters are about enjoying life and how God is just a great God! So, please, feel free to graze and enjoy!

In case you decide to graze, please note that each chapter title is followed by a parenthetical reference to a specific *type of towel* (shown in parentheses under the chapter title). These types of towels suggest the depth of the material contained in the chapter. (For example, the first chapter, "A Book I'd Like to Write," is identified as "Hand Towel.")

There are four types of towels, each of which is described below:

"Bath Towel" indicates a chapter where the contents are *very serious*, and may be difficult for some to handle. An example of very serious is the time a young man at the Boys and Girls Club with tears welling in his eyes said, "I like it when my father gets drunk because that is the only time he talks with me."

"Beach Towel" indicates a chapter where the contents are light-hearted, fun, enjoyable reading. An example is when I mistakenly used the Ladies Room at a local Walmart.

"Hand Towel" indicates a chapter where the contents are serious, but easy to handle. An example is when Jesus was watching me use six carpenter levels to create a level trench, and then cheerfully tapped me on the shoulder and asked me "What does water do?"

"Wash Cloth" indicates a chapter where the contents are a series of quick reads; one can take a minute or however much time one may wish to spend. The book is full of these quick reads.

Rest assured none of the stories are about "towels."

Part Dos y Medio:
Thanks To Gary Larson, Scott Adams, Bill Watterson, and Walt Kelly

In this Part Dos y Medio, I thank Messrs. Larson, Adams, Watterson, and Kelly for reinforcing that I need not worry about being *correct* in how I wrote this book. I also need not worry about proper grammar or real words; witness the onslaught of this by recent Presidents of the United States. I also learned that a chapter *can* be half a page.

Three of these authors taught me that it is highly enjoyable to nourish one's avant-garde thoughts. For doing this, they have each been presumably highly rewarded with fame, fortune, women, wine and all that other so-called good stuff with which celebrities are rewarded.

Yet I also feel rewarded in my own plebian fashion.

When I feel I have accomplished something of great value, I typically reward myself with a hot cup of tea accompanied by two biscotti. Sometimes I reward myself with a double sip of Kirkland Irish Whiskey, or that other great deal, the Costco Kirkland Vodka (in 2020, each only $19.99 for 1.75 liter), or, if I deem my creation to be really, really good stuff, I'll make the sip with Bulleit Rye, or, Woodford Reserve Bourbon, or Bombay Sapphire. Once in a great while, I may also pull out the ole martini shaker in which to make myself a Crown Royal Rye Manhattan, complete with bitters. Oh, my!

The fourth author, Walt Kelly, does not seem to have been as avant-garde as the other three; he was much more "relatable." Because of his down-to-earth-yness, Mr. Kelly has probably been the creator of more oft-repeated quotes than the other three. For example, "We have met the enemy and he is us," or, "Don't take life so serious. It ain't nohow permanent," or, "Having lost sight of our objectives, we redoubled our efforts," or, "Looking back on things, the view always improves," or finally, "If you can't win, don't join them; learn how to lose."

Setting aside the popularity of these quotes, the "bestest" quote for me was from Albert telling Pogo *"I can't go to a fire with a green stomach."* (Please note this has no special meaning; I just like to repeat it, sort of *meiguanxi* (in Mandarin), *"It is of no consequence."* ☺)

INTRODUCTION

It is challenging to discuss the topic of suicide *and* balance such a complex subject with reassuring words and light-hearted, entertaining stories. This book does it! (There are very powerful words in this writing, such that I wondered if I dare ask, "Did *I* write this?" ... the answer, a clear "No, you only held the pencil.")

This book is intended as a journey, an exploration into a world where according to studies, "over 50 percent of all Americans will struggle with mental health issues during their life time ... every one reading this ... (has) ... dealt with anxiety or depression ... or knows someone who has." This reflects a sad fact, that "... 60 men are lost to suicide every hour across the world; in the US this accounts for more than 37,700 men who die by suicide each year."

This book is about how one person was guided by God and the four angels God sent me to be able to share with you why life is worth staying alive and how I have learned to pass on God's unconditional love in fun ways.

My experiences reach out lovingly to anyone in the throes of suicidal depression and *especially to anyone struggling with how to better understand why a person may be in this deep doo-doo.* It tells what worked for me *and* what did not.

In order to balance the serious topic of suicide, I encourage you to leisurely stroll through the Table of Contents. You will find many inviting and uplifting stories ... and so I invite you to join me on an incredible journey, a journey guided by God, a really amazing journey!

A Book I'd Like To Write

(Hand Towel)

I'm glad I had years of Dad's papers to go through after he died.

Had I not had the benefit of *having* to go through just about every single item in Dad's boxes of *stuff*, my lasting memories of him would have been based on our interactions in his later years during which he did some crazy stuff. Fortunately for me, going through Dad's papers helped me to see him through different eyes.

Dad was a poster child for that old joke where a young man tells his friends that he "wished to die just like his grandfather, with his eyes closed and a big smile on his face, not like the five passengers in his car."

Pop's last days were in a little town of 5,000 population where he lived his 90+ years. It is also a town where he would drive me crazy as he pulled on to Main Street, his *boat* of a car taking up a portion of two lanes as he pulled out of his favorite restaurant's parking lot.

As Dad pulled out of the parking lot directly into the street, I often had to say, "Pop, be careful, there are cars coming." He would confidently reply that "everyone in town knows my car, and they will wait for me," suggesting they would give him the right of way.

For Pop, this was a very familiar movement since he typically ate three meals a day at Rudy's Restaurant ever since Mom died years earlier.

The familiarity extended to his eating habits. As a result, when one of the restaurant staff saw Dad's car turning left from Main Street into their parking lot, the word would be passed around and they would begin preparing *his usual*, be it breakfast, lunch or dinner. Dad also had two or three favorite tables, and one preferred server. Others might get his coffee and water at the table but *she* did the waiting on him.

His favorite table was just to the right as one walked into the large dining room. From there he could *stand guard* and be ready to greet others, although he really liked it when others would greet him. He was frequently interrupted by someone, usually a male in his 40s to 60s, who would either first greet Dad, or start by saying to his dinner companions, "Come here, I want you to meet my Scout Master; he taught me so many of the things that I've passed on to you." (Dad's affection for *his* Boy Scouts was so complete that he asked one of them to be part of the church service for his funeral.)

This affection from old friends was a clear highlight in his life as he neared and passed his 80s. The only other time I recall that slight smile on his face was when someone he knew in town, who looked down on my Dad because he had been a mail carrier (on a bicycle in his day), would get his come-uppance. This would occasionally occur when one of these "Too-Important-To-Mingle-With-The-Little-People" (TITMWTLP) would be sitting at their table waiting for their food to be served, and observing that within five minutes of Dad's arrival at his table, he was being served.

Overheard from the table with the TITMWTLP would be, "Why did he get served before us? He just got here." ☺

Dad's driving habits were not particularly comforting to me since Dad had totaled two cars in the two years after Mom died. My concern was so great that my wife and I moved to New Mexico certain that after the second accident, he would lose his driver's license and we would have to be nearby to help him get around.

As it turned out the first accident occurred on Indian land and his accident was never reported to the State.

The second accident occurred on a stretch of the first four-lane highway built in the United States. It consisted of four, wide, travel lanes with an even wider median separating the north and south bound lanes and 30-foot rights-of-way on the outside of the travel lanes, resulting in absolutely no hidden obstructions.

The accident happened when "a big ole hay baler" suddenly pulled out "right in front of him onto the highway at a high rate of speed," as *he* was traveling "safely and at a low speed." (In case you're not familiar with this farm equipment, it actually travels very slowly, certainly not fast enough to *suddenly* pull in front of anyone very quickly, leaving them no room to avoid them.)

When Pop went to court for his second accident, the presiding judge looked up as Dad walked into the court room and said, "Judge C. ... it's good to see you. What are you doing here?" (Dad had been a municipal judge for a short time in our home town.)

The police officer involved with Dad's case overheard the Judge's comment and wisely decided that it would be a waste of his valuable time to wait for this case to be called. So when Dad's case came up, the Judge called for the police officer. Understandably the officer did not present himself having left the court room.

"Well, it looks like there is no one here to present your case. Why don't you just pay the court costs ... and I'll see you tomorrow at the Donut King."

Bottom line: no tickets for either accident and therefore no "marks" on his driving record.

And so, "Everyone in town recognizes my car and they will wait for me" made perfect sense.

Do I Really Have To Go Through Every Sheet Of Paper?

In going through Dad's files after he died, I had two early reactions: first, that man never threw anything away! Things like his monthly calendars, 30-40 years of them! I repeat, *monthly* calendars! My second reaction was, "Do I really have to go through every sheet of paper?"

One would reasonably think, "It should not take too much time to give them a quick glance and if necessary, just rip each page in two and toss them into the waste basket."

As it turned out, that was actually not as reasonable as one might think.

As I began going through the pages, I found lots of information about family members and friends and several strangers.

I found out, for instance, that "back in the day," getting a social security number was not as important to most folks as it is today. Therefore, many people did not bother to get a social security number. However, Dad would help them get those papers. Apparently he discovered that some (probably relatives) still did not see that as important and would not hold on to their numbers. They would come back later and ask Dad if he remembered their numbers. As a result, Pop kept their social security numbers in his monthly calendar along with their birth dates. Every new year, he would transpose all that information to the new monthly calendar.

As a result, I realized that I best go through every single page of every single month of every single year to assure there was no other sensitive information in these papers and to assure that those pages were fully shredded.

Dad, I Wish I'd Known You Better

Rather than a tedious effort, this proved to be a remarkable exercise since I soon found that Dad had a remarkable history of doing really amazing things, mostly geared to helping others. Much of this was a surprise to me since I had moved away and not lived at home since grade school. First I was sent to a seminary during my high school years, then a stint in the Air Force, and then I was off to college. After college, I accepted a job out of state and had been out of state since then.

Thus, my awareness of Dad's activities was based on conversations or visits throughout the next 35 years. (I *was* aware that Dad's efforts and contributions had resulted in his being appointed to several Boards of Directors, including the local Hospital and one of the local Banks.) Going through Dad's papers expanded my awareness, however, of who this man was and clearly showed that he was always willing to help others.

One letter in particular caught my attention. It was actually a Thank You note from a young attorney. "Thank you Mr. C., for encouraging me in my career. I am now a very successful attorney."

To this day I have no idea who that person was, or is, other than he was one of many who wrote my Dad a Thank You note, possibly one of his beloved Boy Scouts. This was only one of many surprising notes I found in my father's files.

Other impressive items in the volumes of files were minutes of trials when he had presided over many cases as a municipal judge. Granted these were not earth shaking cases since he was a municipal judge in a little town of 5,000 folks; however, many of these cases could have been out of the files of Judge Judy, often seemingly petty. But I found that this farm boy who barely graduated from his local high school had on many occasions presided over these trials with much more demeanor and clarity than Judge Judy often does. Certainly, he treated every one with much more respect.

Reading these minutes of the trials, I found that my Dad, a non-attorney, nonetheless reasoned successfully with the best lawyers. I found notes where I recognized the attorneys representing the defendants and saw how their arrogance in dealing with this "hick-town judge" put them right in the cross-hairs of my Dad's extremely reasoned positions.

When reading some of this, I thought to myself, I'm glad that I inherited some of Dad's genes; I believe he was proud of me for that. There were so many times when, like most of us at some point in our lives, we have had to deal with some arrogant person. Irrespective of the experiences which I had, circumstances frequently guided me to manage an office or a project team consisting of persons with expertise in specific fields in which I had no experience or knowledge. At those times, I had to use my intuition based primarily on empirical situations to comfortably verify that what the team was doing was appropriate.

Occasionally, I would have to deal with *professionals* who knew that they were much more experienced than I in their particular field and therefore felt that they could talk down to me, assuming that they would therefore be able to *convince* me, and if necessary *shame* me into acquiescing to their demand/point of view. Fortunately, I had learned how to intuitively question the data or conclusions thus verifying accuracy as well as red-flagging "BS" that needed to be re-done.

The bottom line is that I gained a full appreciation for showing full and clear respect for others, like my father. The times when I forgot to show respect, I found myself to have been a total fool. Thanks Dad for that essential lesson.

Which leads me to my final conclusion, *"Dad, I wish I'd known you better!"*

Angels We Have Heard On High,
Angels We Have Felt On Earth

(Hand Towel)

What I describe next are 10 (ten) angels who have popped in and out of my life. These angels are different from the persons described in the chapter, "Brief Encounters," since those persons are in my life now only as a pleasant memory.

These 10 angels on the other hand have permanent rent-free lodging in my heart as long as they wish. They came into my life in such a way that I owe them a debt of gratitude.

A Little Bit Of Heaven Here On Earth

Six of my angels continue to affect me in a way where I experience what I imagine to be "a little bit of heaven here on earth." They bring me a smile each time I think of them, especially when I need a break from the heavy things sometimes swirling around me. An added bonus, "It *don't* cost a thing. What a deal!"

I have not met these six angels in person. I don't even know the names of five of them, but boy do they help me re-gain an upbeat attitude every time I think of them. I would not be surprised if you have also come across some of them yourself. Just google: "Blakely and her first ice cream," or "two little boys running towards one another," or, "Chinese grandfather dancing the Chinese Shuffle with his two granddaughters."

The first one of these is a nine-month old, little bundle of pure joy, a classic little cutie; little Blakely first hit the airwaves via the internet where she is seen enjoying her first taste of ice cream. Her sweet baby innocence brings such joy that I can clearly see her whenever I think of her even without my computer.

She bites into an ice cream cone held by one of her parents. As she lets the ice cream melt into her little mouth, her little brown eyes grow wide and she simultaneously grabs the cone and digs her chubby, little fingers into the scoop of rocky road vanilla ice cream. Hilarious! Often when I am feeling overwhelmed, I go to the internet and play that scene. It instantly brings a bit of heaven into my life.

Another example of pure, innocent joy is where two 2-year old boys are running towards one another on a sidewalk as fast as their chubby little legs can carry them. One with GGT, the other having to sunbathe in order to get any tan whatsoever. (GGT is an acronym I use for anyone who has a God Given Tan, as in having a darker skin than those of us who have to work hard to get "a nice tan.")

Neither of them is aware of the difference in the color of their skin, just happy to see one another after a long weekend apart. They are both stout little guys who run hard into one another without either one getting knocked down by the force of their joyful exuberance in seeing their BFF. Their mutual genuine affection is so pure and unconditional!

The last google to which I refer is the one to which I turn most often because it is full of pure warmth in a most subtle way.

This is a YouTube video of a 90-year old Chinese grandfather going through a 60-second shuffle dance with his two granddaughters, one about five years old, the other about eight years old.

Dressed in a black sweater and black pants with white gloves, he is very stoic in his facial gestures.

On the other hand, the two little girls are quite animated in their black leggings and red tops. The older granddaughter is bouncing around so enthusiastically that her pony tail and her pig tails seem to give lift to her dance. The black tassels on her black boots add movement to her joyous dancing while the red blouse she is wearing bounces around as she moves, her dancing so alive and vigorous.

Her younger sister, with only a single pony tail, is just a little bit less fluid than she. What is extra engaging about the younger one is how she keeps looking at her grandpa, who is dancing between the two girls, to assure she stays in step with him. At one point, he gets a half-step off their choreographed dance; she immediately adjusts her step to be in tune with his. What loving, heartwarming energy!

This one-minute video is full of brisk, gleeful, carefree, enchanting, cheerful, smoothly choreographed movement! Would that the whole world had such simple, genuine, innate affection for one another!

A Debt Of Gratitude

To the following four angels, I owe more than a debt of gratitude; I owe them my continuing to be alive. There have probably been more angels who have helped me continue to live, but these are the ones of whom I am most aware, ones who were sent to pull me out of the very deep holes of depression into which I had fallen.

They were sent to me by God at the lowest points in my life, a time when I was prepared to "transition out of this world." Two of them were sent as I was in the final steps, just before "the transition."

The first angel called as I was ready to take my last step out of this life. (I had visited her at her insistence the weekend before.) She was now calling me with tears in her voice. Her brother having taken his life years earlier and her sister-in-law having recently died, she was in a very delicate state of mind and must have picked up hints that maybe I was also "on the brink" of passing on.

In this case, she did not do a lot of listening as she was pleading with me not to do what her younger brother had done, unexpectedly take his life. "I don't want to lose you, too," she cried. Out of respect for her, I compromised with my inclination and the thought, "Okay, not today." And so, "Okay, not today" eventually turned into "Okay, not this month" over and over.

The second angel popped into my life in such a way that it had to be a miracle. The call came from a posh art gallery on Rodeo Drive in Beverly Hills. I was living in Tucson at the time. A call from Beverly Hills?

Part of the reason why I attribute this entire experience with my second angel to be a miracle is that, for an unknown reason, I answered the phone ... something I had not done for several weeks.

Although I was a bit busy at the time, I put the razor blade down to pick up the telephone.

The voice on the other end said, "Hi, I'm Amy P. I'm calling you from 'xyz Art Gallery' in Beverly Hills. You were here last summer and expressed interest in the LeRoy Neiman elephant painting, 'Elephant Charge.' I'm sorry that we have not called you since you were here in June but ..."

The voice suddenly stopped talking and she said, "You're not okay, are you?"

I burst into tears.

Amy listened and cared.

This whole series of unbelievable events began when my oldest daughter invited my ex's daughter to come visit her for a week in LA. My ex for some unexplainable reason agreed, but only on the condition that I take her daughter to LA.

When we arrived in LA, my daughter asked "The Bean" what she would like to do while she was there. HB being a wonderfully precocious 13 year old immediately said, "Go shopping on Rodeo Drive."

And so there we were walking down Rodeo Drive when we passed a window with paintings by LeRoy Neiman. One riveting painting in the middle of the display was his "Elephant Charge." Having admired his work, I stopped and suggested we go in.

For another unexplainable reason, the gallery owner approached us and after talking with us briefly invited us into a private viewing room where he brought in several paintings, one being the "Elephant Charge." When he asked if I were interested, I said something about how terrific it was but knowing that there was no way I could afford it, I mentioned having a friend in San Diego who was also into elephants. I knew that she could afford it for her condo in La Jolla. I took his card and apparently left my name and Tucson telephone number with him.

Five months later, the phone rang and I found myself talking with Amy, a total stranger, who was calling me from the Beverly Hills art gallery. Bizarrely, the visit to the art gallery had occurred back in June; it was now November. My being on Rodeo Drive for the first and only time in my life was already extraordinary. And now a phone call? Why the phone call at this moment?

Amy, not knowing me, was genuinely concerned for me. She cared enough to forego the sale of the painting (the original purpose of her call) and instead focused on me. From 500 miles away, she had the ability to "feel" over the phone a stranger's hurt and struggles.

Over the next few months, Amy and I developed a human-caring relationship that steered me to put away all my razor blades for a long time and instead to focus on living rather than on "transitioning."

Years later, I again slowly slipped back into full despair. During this time, I met a woman (about my father's age) who *guided* me to my third angel. I do not recall the specific circumstances under which I met this woman, nor do I recall *why* or *what* I said to her that moved her to suggest that I make an appointment to see "G. N." a kinesiologist, who turned out to be my third angel. I had never heard of a kinesiologist, but once again I was inexplicably guided to call her for an appointment. "G. N." not only helped stabilize me over time but became a good friend of mine (as well as a friend of the fourth angel who God sent me).

The fourth angel I had met 20 years earlier in Kansas. Now I was in Arizona and she was in California. When we met earlier, she was married and I was with the woman with whom I thought I would spend the rest of my life. As the years went by, we both moved several times and became single. For again some reason only God was privy to, we exchanged birthday cards every year, and thus we kept in touch with one another.

Over time, we refreshed our friendship, eventually she becoming my Mary of whom one can read in many of these chapters. Mary and I celebrated our twentieth wedding anniversary last year. She is my pillar now; brought together by God in another unbelievable miracle. (Read the chapter, "Miracles.")

Brief Encounters

(Beach Towel)

Many people come into our lives for brief moments. All encounters make a difference, yet some stand out because they were extra special, and for some reason they made enough of an impact on our lives that we remember them years later with a smile, or, with gratitude for having had the good fortune of having them in our lives even if only for a brief time.

This is a small tribute to a few of these special people who made an extra special impression on my life. There is the real possibility that these brief encounters may be meaningful only to me, but I think you'll like these people too. ☺

There are so many more that I could have included: Donna in Kansas; Donna in Oklahoma; Larry, Jan, Jill, John, Dianne, Gerry, Ross, Doug, Gary, and Annie in Arizona; John, Pete, Lyle, Filomena, and Delia in San Diego.

Beth In Tucson

One of my favorite eating places when I lived in Tucson was Jerry Bob's. At the time as a bachelor, I often went to Jerry Bob's on Friday afternoons where they served a delicious all-you-can-eat fried catfish. When my Pop was in town, I took him there a lot since he loved anything deep fried. [He had one of those appetites where he would ask that they deep fry the *already* deep fried fish ... just kidding! He was sort of like my wife's grandmother who *loved* butter and would ask for buttered bread and upon being served would immediately say, "Oh, come on, put some *more* butter on that bread!"]

Years after Mary and I had moved to Albuquerque, we happened to be in Tucson on a Friday. Since we had already sated Mary's need for the enchiladas from Poco and Mom's Restaurant, she had no choice but to acquiesce to my choice for dinner, Jerry Bob's delicious all-you-can-eat fried catfish.

On that occasion, the server was a young lady who was clearly not moving very fast and who sweetly continued to apologize that it was taking her "so long" to get something for us. (We learned later that Beth was dealing with a health issue that was affecting her.)

We told her, "Don't worry, we are in no hurry."

When we finished eating, Mary walked over to her and gave her one of our "passing-on" cards, telling her to open it up after she got home from work. (Note: One of the ways that Mary and I thank God is to pass on God's bounty to us in the form of little greeting cards with $20 dollar bills in them, and the words, "Remember that God's love is always with us. Pass it on!")

Beth did not wait to open the envelope, and before we could walk to the front of the restaurant to pay at the cash register, she rushed up to us with tears in her eyes asking if she could give us a hug.

This story does not end there.

Ten years later, we happened to be in Tucson again on a Friday. This time, however, it was my wife who suggested going to Jerry Bob's.

And there she was, the same woman we had seen ten years earlier. When she saw us, she walked over to ask us what we would like.

Before ordering, Mary said to her, "You probably don't remember us. It's been about ten years since we were last here."

Beth, with swelling tears, said, "Oh, I remember you. You gave me that lovely card with money in it."

There had to have been hundreds of customers since we were last there. A clearly special brief encounter; make that two very special encounters, ten years apart!

Lorraine In Florence

On one of my wife's special birthdays, she chose as her special gift a trip along the Oregon coast. After flying into Eugene, we got a rental car and headed to the coast having made reservations for three nights at the River House Inn in Florence. As usual, I took advantage of the free breakfast the next morning, allowing my wife to take a longer time to sleep without my making unwanted noise in the room.

The breakfast area consisted of two rooms, one a large room upstairs where most people took their food to eat. The other was a small room downstairs where the food was served. It had three small tables, each seating 1-3 people.

I grabbed the table where only one person could comfortably sit without obstructing the path so that the lady attending to the coffee making could get to the small fridge where they had boiled eggs, yogurt, and milk.

I struck up a friendly conversation with the lady attendant, a woman about my wife's age. I pondered about the fact that my wife was enjoying a really special *first-class* trip and this lady had to work, first as the breakfast attendant and then as part of the housekeeping crew. The fact that she was working at her age, clearly spoke out that she was obviously not in "the top 1%."

Since I was not in a hurry, I took a book to read. To make sure I was not tying up needed tables, I asked her to let me know if she needed the table for others.

She smilingly told me that there were many tables available upstairs and to take my time.

As I observed her coming and going, I noticed that she was basically a beautiful soul, being very friendly while assisting everyone with any minute thing, making waffles for well-coiffed women and getting coffee for a male who could have been her son. The entire time she was pleasant with everyone, including those who seemed to treat her as "just one of the help."

At one point when there was no crowd, she came over and asked me if I would like more coffee, or, maybe I would like her to make a waffle for me.

I smiled and told her that I was fine and if she was not busy to just take a break and sit down, which she gladly did. Running up and down the stairs at her age was I am sure tiring.

She asked politely if I were there with someone, and when I mentioned my wife's birthday, she happily burst out, "It's my birthday also!" It turned out her birthday was a day after my wife's birthday, born the same year.

For her birthday, one of those milestone birthdays that end in a "0," she said her husband had told her to pack an overnight bag, but would not tell where they were going. She guessed they might be going into Eugene for the night.

When I told my wife about "Lorraine" and that her birthday was the day after Mary's, she suggested we run to the local store and get her a birthday card.

The next morning, I gave Lorraine the Happy Birthday card. My wife had put $70 in it, that being a number special to both of their birthdays.

I told Lorraine not to open it until after she got home from work. Of course she didn't wait. She walked out of the breakfast room and within a few minutes came back inside with a big smile. I got one of the warmest hugs that "a stranger" could ever share with someone else.

That being the day we were checking out, I told her that I wanted Mary to meet her. She said, "You betcha! I owe *her* a hug!"

We think of Lorraine every September now, and send her a "Happy Birthday" prayer each year.

Linda on the Big Island

This brief encounter is one I remember for the simplicity of the encounter.

Linda worked the Big Island Breakfast. This was clearly the most popular eating place at the Hilton Waikoloa, seating well over 200 persons at one time.

The restaurant was only open for their big breakfast buffet which was quite a spread serving a fantastic variety of island specials along with the traditional breakfast items found back on the mainland.

But this story is not about the food. It is about a very simple, sweet lady named Linda.

Being there for a week, Mary and I struck up a conversation with her. She was a lovely older woman. Since the breakfast buffet was not inexpensive and people were 100% tourists to the island as we were, I assume it was a good gig since people on vacation supposedly are more free with their tips. Nonetheless, Linda and the other servers fully earned any tips they received always assuring that diners had everything they wanted.

Linda was especially attentive as the days went on, even indulging us in conversation more personal than the traditional diner/server interactions.

Each day we shared personal stories, none of which are relevant to this account. (And yes, we were generous with our tips, but Linda was also generous with the forbidden "take outs" for my wife when Mary did not join me, e.g., a glass of fat-free milk to take back to the room.)

On the second to the last day that we were there, I gave Linda one of our "passing-on" envelopes on top of the $20 tip. As Mary and I always do, we told her that it was for *after work* and not to open it til then. Linda was the first person to agree not to open it until later. She said she was going to save it to open on Christmas day since she was spending Christmas by herself that year. (It was mid-December when we were there.) Wow, a big lump materialized in our hearts. Fortunately, we had made this "passing-on" card a bit more special for her and had put a $50 bill in it. When she told us that she was going to save it for Christmas, we gave her another "passing-on" card so that she could open *something that day.* (I would not be surprised if that second envelope also went into her Christmas gift box.)

Alyssa In Pismo Beach

The brief encounter with Alyssa is one that I will always remember.

Alyssa was a 20ish-year old young lady with one of those weird-to-an-old-guy hair styles, shaved down to the skull on one side, with bright colorings on the remainder.

She was working at the registration desk of a charming hotel overlooking the Pacific Ocean in which we were going to spend a week. At first sight she appeared to be someone who did not wish to have to socialize with some old guy (me). As it turned out, Alyssa went *above and beyond* to make our stay at the Lighthouse Suites a truly memorable one.

A flyer, "An Evening With Garrison Keillor," was pinned on the wall behind her with an announcement that Garrison Keillor was going to perform the next evening at Questa College in neighboring San Luis Obispo. Having been a longtime fan of his "Prairie Home Companion" radio shows on PBS, I immediately became excited and wondered aloud if at such a late time we could get tickets.

Long story short, it was a sold-out performance, but Alyssa offered to call the college and see what she could do for us.

A few minutes after we had unpacked the car, our room phone rang. It was Alyssa with an unexpectedly thrilled voice, "Guess what? I found you two seats but they are up front, and you will have to drive over to San Luis Obispo today to be sure to get the tickets." What a sweetie; we *certainly* did not mind!

The next night's performance was typical Keillor, wrinkled suit, dry humor. As it turned out, the tickets we paid for included an after-performance cocktail party at which we got to talk with the star! (See "Thots, Random - My Baby's," "Mary's Magical Maxims, I Have No Idea Why I Said That" about Mr. Keillor.)

The next day, I gave Alyssa a thank you card with a $50 bill for going out of her way to get those tickets for us.

The last day before we checked out, there was an envelope on our door. Inside was a letter from Alyssa telling us that she was on her way to college in southern California where she was going to pursue a degree in film-making. She said that what she was going to do as part of her college class was to script a movie about me. She asked who I would like to play me. She suggested DeNiro. I think I joked that while I absolutely loved DeNiro, that I thought it should be someone more handsome, someone like Paul Newman. I've forgotten her response but what I do recall was that she was a "Poster Child" for not judging someone by their looks; *she was* a very beautiful young lady inside and out.

Alyssa, I have lost track of you. If anyone knows how to get hold of her, please let me know. I would love to find out about her successes and, of course, whether she ever did a movie about me. ☺

Dianne In Port Orford

The "brief encounter" with Dianne occurred over a two and a half year period.

It began when my mother-in-law (I'll refer to her as Mom) who lived in Oregon at the time responded to our question of what would she like to do to celebrate her upcoming 90th birthday. She said she would love to visit the town of Brookings, located just north of the California/Oregon state line. Having asked her several months before her birthday, we had ample time to make it a special trip.

Investigating the optional itineraries from Roseburg where she lived at the time, I came across the town of Port Orford, a few hours north of Brookings. I also noted that there was a restaurant in Port Orford called "The Crazy Norwegian."

"What a discovery," I thought, "Mom having been married to a Norwegian, what a perfect place to see about planning a special surprise 90th birthday meal at The Crazy Norwegian!"

My first call to The Crazy Norwegian was answered by the owner, Dianne.

When she answered the phone, I said, "Hi, I'm Fil. I'm calling from Albuquerque." Dianne's reply was a good natured, "Well, good for you!"

(In googling the towns along the way, I had checked out the various "yelp" reviews and found that there had been many customers "put off" by what they considered impolite banter from the owner. For me, I found Dianne's natural exuberance delightfully welcoming in a very inimitable way. Thus, when she said, "Well, good for you," I absolutely knew that we *had to* plan a special birthday celebration for Mom at The Crazy Norwegian.)

After that initial call, I had to call her several times to work out the details in order to make the celebration special plus we were going to stop there on our way from Roseburg to Brookings that same day. Each time I called (Dianne had given me her cell phone number), I laughingly said, "Hi Dianne, this is Fil from Albuquerque."

Long story sort of short: we worked up a very special surprise celebration focusing on Mom's favorite dessert. Unfortunately, family issues scuttled the entire trip just days before we were to arrive in Oregon. I profusely apologized to Dianne and offered to pay for any expenses she may have incurred. She refused the offer.

Fast forward eighteen months ...

This time it was one of those special birthdays for my wife. When I asked Mary what she would like to do for her special birthday, she said she would like to travel the coast of Oregon.

With this in mind, we flew into Eugene, rented a car and planned to arrive in Port Orford on Mary's birthday. The Redfish Loft where we were to stay had a very fancy, highly acclaimed restaurant where we planned to celebrate Mary's birthday the day we arrived. Unfortunately, the restaurant made a schedule change the week before we arrived and decided to close the restaurant on Tuesdays, starting on the day we were arriving.

Port Orford is a very small town, less than a 1,000 population. However it is well situated in terms of travel along the coast. The Redfish Loft where we were staying happened to be a block from The Crazy Norwegian. (So, guess where we had Mary's special birthday meal.)

The Crazy Norwegian is a small restaurant with about 15 tables. (The scrumptious food and rustic ambiance are "worth going out of the way" just to savor both.)

We were *pointed to* a table in the back room. (This *is* an informal place, along the lines of Dianne's greeting to me two years earlier, "Hi, I'm Fil, from Albuquerque." Dianne: "Well, good for you.")

Dianne was not at the restaurant when we arrived but we were told that she should be there soon. We went ahead and ordered our food. About twenty minutes later, an SUV pulled into the driveway. I could see that a dog had accompanied the driver and thus assumed that this was likely Dianne.

When we asked the server if that were Dianne, would she tell her that we would like to say "Hi!" to her. (I was reluctant to do this because of the fiasco two years earlier when Dianne had really gone out of her way to do something extra special for Mom, and then we had been forced to cancel the trip at the last minute. Adding to my reluctance, Dianne had not replied when I emailed her and left a telephone message that we were finally coming to eat at her restaurant, and that I was bringing a true Norwegian, my wife, for *her* special birthday. I therefore had assumed that she was upset about what had transpired two years earlier.)

After a few minutes of saying hello to several locals, she came over to our table to see what we wanted. She greeted us with a quizzical, "Can I help you?"

My wife blurted out, "Hi Dianne, This is Fil ... from Albuquerque."

Dianne's reaction floored me, almost literally, as she lunged at me and gave me one of the best hugs I've ever received from a non-family member.

It was such a pleasure to finally put a face (and a hug) to the wonderful *stranger* who two years earlier went *Above and Beyond* to plan a special birthday celebration meal for my wife's 90-year old mother "just because." God bless you Dianne. What a special person you are!

An Ice Cream Parlor In Florence and Rose In Port Orford

Unlike the other brief encounters described above, this is a brief encounter which I wish had not happened.

This one resulted in a critical "Lesson Learned" for my wife and me.

Basically, the lesson is that one cannot usually go back and *right a wrong*.

My wife and I walked into an ice cream parlor in Florence, where we had experienced two wonderful days.

One of the special experiences I promised my wife on this very special birthday trip of hers was to get her as much ice cream as possible. In this case there was a much-heralded ice cream parlor in town. After having a nice lunch on the harbor, we walked across the street to enjoy *a little treat.*

A group of six or seven people with a couple of kids and several adults walked out as we walked in, each "yumming" at the ice cream waffle or ice cream dish they had.

When we walked in, we immediately began looking at the various kinds of ice cream they offered. As we did so, we noticed a fly buzzing around the inside of the display case. When the one worker on duty walked over to help us, we somewhat nonchalantly joked about the fly. It was then we noticed his "hard-lived" face, one that showed no interest in any type of humor and almost disdain for us pointing out the fly.

We got the message: "order your ice cream and get the heck out of here."

When he gave us our change, he did so putting the money down next to the Tips jar.

My reaction was one akin to *forget you* if you think we are going to give you a tip after your nasty attitude.

We walked out. When we got back to our room, we discussed how un-Christian our actions were. We determined that the next day as we drove out of town, we would drive by the Ice Cream Parlor and give that man one of our "passing-on" envelopes with a $20 bill.

To our disappointment, the man was not there and was not scheduled to be back in the near future. It was too late to *right our wrong*. A hard lesson learned.

This lesson was magnified when we met Rose in Port Orford. While in Port Orford, we ate a couple of times in the restaurant that was part of the lodging we were renting for three days. Rose was a server at this restaurant.

Rose was a very sweet young lady, quiet yet friendly. She oozed warmth and caring for others. She was a person who walked in with a visibly positive attitude. She likely would have given the man at the ice cream parlor in Florence a big smile that would have changed his nasty attitude into a civil one. We have since warned ourselves to be more like Rose; it should not be about whether someone *deserves our smile*, but rather whether they *need a smile*.

Since that hard lesson, we have worked hard to walk always showing love or at least respect, rather than waiting to react with love or respect *if they deserve it.* As we learned that day, it is sometimes too late to pass on God's love, and so we are training ourselves to be more like Rose and walk around with what we call "The Rose Bowl Of Love."

Cynthia In Sacramento

Cynthia is an old acquaintance of Mary's. Long story very short: I met Cynthia on one of our trips to Sacramento. For some reason, she gave me a book that has had a major impact on my life and my relationship with God, *The Shack.* (I have to date read the book line by line 11 times. Each time, I have found something significant that has permanently affected my life. This was a truly special gift. Thank you, Cynthia.)

Oftentimes, one single, simple gesture will inspire a permanent impact on another's life.

Don and Jane On The Train Across Canada

Don and Jane are two of the most beautiful and fun people with whom one would want to have an encounter! We met them on an incredibly memorable five-day trip on the VIA Rail from Toronto to Vancouver, BC.

Our encounter began on the first day of the five-day train trip across the stunning landscape of Canada.

Mary and Jane were sitting in the Park Car (aka the Dome Car or the Scenic Car). They were busy talking, getting to know one another and observing the fantastic Canadian landscapes go by. My wife was wearing a big, floppy hat to protect her skin from the sun coming in through the windows in the Dome Car.

Suddenly, my wife heard a voice behind her asking "Did you *actually* pay for that hat?" Jane turned and admonished Don, "Oh Don, stop that." This was the first of many *can't stop laughing episodes* over the next few days with our new-found traveling companions, Don and Jane. (Mary and I still tease one another with "Did you *actually* pay for that hat?")

The encounters with Don and Jane were nonstop fun and full of laughter on this train ride. We enjoyed one another so much that we had lunch and dinner together every day.

At one of our dinners, we were laughing so hard that a young server came over to us and said, "Can I be your server next time? You all are having so much fun!"

One of the more memorable experiences was at our last meal before Don and Jane got off the train at Jasper in order to catch the train to Saint George. We had been advised that soon after lunch, those departing would be given an hour to get their luggage and get off the train, so there was no hurry when we pulled into the station.

We finished our lunch in the same jovial way in which we had enjoyed all of our meals in the last few days with the quiet, smiling Jane and the gregarious, always joking Don.

Before they left, I had decided to put on a serious "facial gesture;" I said in a serious business voice, "See all those people standing out there on the platform waiting to get on the train?"

"Well, we would appreciate it if you would pick out two or three couples for us to interview so that we can select one to be our 'meal friends' as you have been with us."

I continued, "Actually, we would like you to select a couple who are: (1) funny, but not as funny as we are; (2) interesting, but not as interesting as we are; and (3) good looking, but not as good looking as we are."

Before I could go on, Jane piped in, "Is that how you selected us?" We all laughed heartily for the last time together.

Don, unbeknownst to us at the time was on his "one last train ride before I die" trip. He has since moved on from making us laugh and feel better about life on this earth to entertaining lots of strangers (strangers not for long) in Heaven for the last five years.

God bless you, Jane. Don, when you are looking over Jane's shoulder, give us a nudge also.

Aunt Beatrice In Gallup

Another always-ready-with-a-big-smile was my Aunt Beatrice. It never failed that when we ran into one another at family gatherings (with the usual large crowds) I would feel a tug from across the room and when I looked up, there would be my gorgeous grinning auntie still talking with others but smiling in my direction. As I traversed the crowd to work my way over to her, she stood there looking at me with that same engaging smile until we were able to share a wonderfully warm hug.

Partially for this reason, I always timed my travels between Albuquerque and Phoenix, Flagstaff or Sedona to coincide with meal time where she and I could "break bread." She loved the Cracker Barrel and after the "meat and taters," she would always pretend to be surprised when I suggested we order dessert. "Dessert, too?" she would exclaim with those big brown eyes of hers suggesting that she was surprised. "Wow!" I miss her smile.

Grace In Arizona

Grace played an important part in my life after my divorce. Although I had known her professionally before my divorce, she told me after we became friends that she did not trust me professionally when we first met since the project for which I was hired as the Project Manager was deemed "questionable" by many in town. Not only was I a consultant, but I was from "out of town." The study itself was deemed to be suspicious by a number of folks in town; this lack of trust included most of the local media.

Fifteen months later, after a very successful study which included many public meetings, several with 500 or more attendees, Grace realized that her preconceived impressions of me, although understandable because of the study, turned out to be untrue.

I do not recall how Grace and I became good friends after my divorce, but the friendship rose to the level of her even asking me to "dog-sit" her dog for a week, the dog being very difficult to befriend especially if one were a male.

Shortly after my divorce, I had sworn that I would never trust another woman again in a personal relationship. The friendship with Grace, however, helped me get past that; and although I remained certain I would never trust another woman again, I realized that I could still be *friends* with a woman.

Part of this "new journey for me" included an invitation to join Grace and some of her very lovely friends (mostly females) on their annual river rafting trip down the Green River. I went even though I did not know how to swim. Moreover, I was only one of four males on the trip; the other three males consisted of the two guides and a husband.

What a joyful experience! As the raft was guided down a Class 4 rapid, I once found myself looking straight down at the raging river.

On this trip, out in the middle of non-urban life with no city lights to blanket the night sky, seeing stars and meteorites every few seconds bolting across the night sky was an irreplaceable occurrence.

Among the numerous matchless experiences on this river rafting trip was being treated to a full rainbow. Not just the crescent shapes we typically see but the entire 360 degree circle!!

Thank you, Grace; you were a good friend at a very difficult and challenging time in my life.

Stephanie In The Vaccination Line

I began this chapter by commenting on how we meet people who make such a profound difference in our lives that we remember them years later. Stephanie is one of those people.

My brief encounter with Stephanie occurred just last week when I was in line for my first Covid-19 vaccination. I am certain that I will remember this encounter for many years to come, although at the time I did not realize that this brief encounter was one which would make a major difference in my life in just a few days.

The day before I met Stephanie I was beginning to question whether "my book" was anything I really wished to pursue through the difficulties of publishing.

I had discovered that the hurdles of writing the book would likely be heavily challenged by the efforts to get the book published. Any excitement that what I had to offer was something that others would be interested in quickly eroded. My reaction was, "Just face it, Fil, you entertained yourself for a few months; time to let it go!" I retreated once again into the bowels of "living in my failures."

However, the day I met Stephanie, as she and I waited in the long line to get vaccinated (about 40 minutes), we began to talk. One topic that came up was my book. Her first question was: "What is the book about?" Gleefully, I told her the title of the book, *Unused Towels;* I also explained the genesis of the title. Stephanie's response seemed to be genuine interest so I told her about the chapter "Embarrassing Moments," specifically, "Why I Have To Wear Sunglasses When I Shop At The Walmart In Los Lunas."

Bottom line: Stephanie's response to what I told her about the book culminated in her asking me when I expected it to be published so that she could be on the lookout for it. I replied that a publishing date was not even on my horizon but that if she wished, she could give me her email address and I would let her know if and when.

The *major difference in my life* that this brief encounter produced was my being encouraged that at least one person besides my Mary might actually be interested in the book. "Maybe I should not be questioning this effort" was the thought in my head when I fell asleep that night. I had come home with a renewed sense of purpose to finish writing this book and a bolstered sense that I need to "Let trust in God control this effort." Thank you Stephanie!

[Mary pointed out to me that I should not have been complaining about all the red lights we had to stop for on the way to the vaccination site. Had we not hit all those red lights, I would not have been favored with a parking spot close to the entrance *and* the exit; a truck pulled out just as we pulled in. Most significantly, I would not have gotten in line next to Stephanie.

Since Stephanie is a nurse, she encouraged me to accept the invitations from the line-monitor volunteers to be taken to the front of the line. (I was walking with a cane and an oxygen tank.) I thanked them each time and said I did not want to cut in front of the line of all those people. After the second "invitation" for me to go up front, Stephanie looked up from her texting and began our unexpected conversation by telling me, "You really should go up there; people won't mind."

Stephanie was there that day because she had missed her earlier opportunity to get vaccinated. And so, those circumstances brought her to be standing next to me.

God builds so many bridges for us, and we are often unaware of those gifts.]

Coffee Talk

(Hand Towel)

One wonderful lesson that my wife and I learned is to begin every day with "Coffee Talk;" it sets a pleasant tone for the day. This has been especially significant after retirement when time has been plentiful, and at a time when couples often get in one another's way.

"Coffee Talk" basically consists of five parts: (1) general conversation – anything not dealing with schedules, (2) conversation regarding tentative plans for the next seven days, and (3) conversation regarding tentative plans for that day. We then conclude our "Coffee Talk" with (4) "three things that bring a smile to our faces," and finally (5) some "Coffee Talk" with God, aka, a prayer.

From there we are *free to go* joyfully hand-in-hand ... in different directions, and take care things that do not include both of us.

This "Coffee Talk" reinforces our marriage at a time when lots of couples grow apart. ("We don't seem to have anything in common anymore," or as the song goes, "You don't bring me flowers, you don't sing me love songs, you hardly talk to me anymore.")

In the process of "Coffee Talk," we've learned a lot about one another, and how each of us came to be the persons we are. Interestingly, instead of wanting to get away from one another, we actually look forward to being together. (*And no, I am not being held prisoner and being forced to say this.* ☺) ... and yes, as I suggested before, we enjoy time to ourselves, but we do so with mutual support. For example, except for "Longmire," "Keeping Up Appearances" on PBS, "Wheel of Fortune," and night-talk shows, we seldom watch the same television programs.

It's crazy; I've never experienced anything as enjoyable as this, and remember we have been together 24/7 for over 20 years!

At a minimum, it cements our bond while it also frees us to go on with our individual plans for the day without guilt for not spending sufficient time with one another. (I consider it a better bonding ritual than what we see among "lions after a family meal," aka "a successful hunt." ☺)

General Conversation

This is a good place to start the "Coffee Talk:" Whatever is on either of our minds is *on the table.* It can be about what happened yesterday, about what was on the "tellie" last night, either the news or a TV program (I love talking about what was on "Blue Bloods," the Reagan family dinners, especially when they pray before dinner, or, when Frank has a drink with his father or with Erin, his daughter.)

Sometimes our general conversation is about something which has been on one of our minds, like "Can you help me order an Ott Light?" or, "Do you think we have enough toilet paper?" (Don't laugh, I am writing this part in 2020; shortage of toilet paper is/was not so funny!)

Again, any topic that does not tie into the other four categories is appropriate, just a calm chat.

Conversation Regarding "Tentative Plans" For The Next Week

Planning our outings has become an efficiency thing recently; we limit our contacts with the world during this 2020 should-not-have-happened pandemic. (I prefer not to call it by its scientific or political label.) Thus, doctor's appointments, runs to Sam's for renewal of prescriptions, purchase of sugar-free popsicles that Albertsons has on sale are all "on the table."

Conversation Regarding "Tentative Plans" For That Day

This conversation only deals with what we will do that day. This is just a leisurely, relaxed dialogue, talking over what we need to do that day with a focus on the day's errands that may require going out. This usually evolves into figuring out whether we are both going out, or, whether I must be the sole *hunter and gatherer*. ☺ Also up for discussion is the timing of these errands so that they are efficient and not stressful.

Sometimes when we have been cooped up for several days, we may decide to "take the long way" on our errands. The drive south from our Post Office in the neighboring town of Bernalillo goes through the Sandia community, still rustic in nature. The views are of riparian cottonwood groves and pastoral pastures feeding horses and cattle, their heads down eating from the wheat and hay fields, with occasional flocks of Canadian and Snow Geese, and seasonal Green Heron and great varieties of ducks.

It also gives my wife the opportunity to talk with the horses in the field. We love to see the horses' heads look up from their grazing as Mary "neighs" to them. Although I must admit that occasionally I feel a bit of jealousy since I was the one who taught her to neigh at the horses. Alas, the horses never stopped foraging to look up at me as they do every time she "talks" with them.

"Three Things That Bring A Smile To Your Face"

The topics for these "three things" change each day; we take turns choosing the themes. Mary chooses them on the even days; I on the odd days.

The areas of conversation are free-wheeling, regarding whatever the TT-ICP ("Three Things" – In Charge Person) designates as the focus.

In the ten-plus years we have been doing this (over 4,000 "three things"), we have never had a problem thinking of something new to offer as that day's "three things" to bring a smile to our faces. Some days we do return to an old topic, not because we have run out of ideas, but because we have more to add since the last time we had that as our subject matter.

Sometimes the topics have been variations of the basic theme, such as, regarding food: best ice cream, best asparagus, best steak, best servers, or "most memorable dining experiences."

The topic of "most memorable dining experiences" merits some explanation. One of these more "favorite food" conversations occurred when Mary and I stopped for lunch at a restaurant in Socorro, New Mexico on our way from Tucson to Albuquerque during the bird watching season when the area is highly populated by older women sans male companions.

The restaurant was full of white haired, female bird-watchers. As we sat looking at the menu we noticed that the server stood patiently waiting to take the orders of the five women seated at the table next to us.

As often happens in a group, there was a lot of chatter even after the server had started taking their orders, someone invariably asking, "What are you having?" seemingly unaware that the server was already taking their orders.

One person replied, "I think I'll have the patty melt."

The server continued with the next person, "What would you like, mam?"

"I think I'll have the chicken tacos."

The previous order immediately changed, "Oh that sounds good; change my patty melt to chicken tacos."

A third voice popped in, "Ooh, that does sound good. Change my salad to the chicken tacos."

At that point, the server abruptly walked away to respond to a group of workers, anxious to get their order in during their brief lunch break.

When the server came back to the women, he began taking their drink orders. He spoke with an exasperated voice and was no longer concerned about being patient. (He had just picked up his tip at another table of white-haired women; that tip consisted of quarters, dimes and nickels, likely less than ten percent of their bill.)

He then came to our table and took our order, with a visibly impatient voice, he blurted out, "Coffee, yes or no? Water, yes or no?"

My wife and I looked at one another and *after* he had brought us our food, my wife turned to me and said in a loud voice, "Tip, yes or no?" ("Sorry, man, we hope you remember the 25% tip *we* left, making up for the less-than-ten-per-cent tip from the ladies, *certainly not* for your service!") Since then when we occasionally encounter a less-than-deserving server, we often say aloud to one another, "Tip, yes or no?"

While this specific "three things" story had a sour side, we focused on the "sweet" side, this time my wife's sense of humor. (We did after all leave a 25% tip.)

The "three things" are often as simple as, "a time when you remember enjoying something in orange," or, "funny times," or, "special times with my dad," or, "fun times with Mary's mother," or, "favorite satires from Dave Barry." It is often "a snap shot" (no long explanation necessary) of the food or drink we remember most, e.g., the grilled garlic from any Pelicans Restaurant, or, the chips and bean dip from Garcia's Restaurant on Peoria Avenue in Phoenix.

Not only has it been enjoyable to remember special moments "down memory lane," but it has also set the tone for having an enjoyable time with each other. [Anyone who has been with a partner (marriage or business) knows that "keeping a bright light" in the relationship is important ... without it the relationship can easily become difficult and routine.]

I highly recommend "Coffee Talk" with "three things." It gives everyone a positive start to the day. We enjoy it so much that we often turn the "three things" into "eight things" in honor of my 80th birthday. Sometimes when we are both stressed because of things going on in our lives or in the world, we will stop and suggest a quick "snap shot" of three things that makes us smile or makes us happy, "snap shot" meaning we don't intend to spend a long time on it. It really works, try it, you'll like it.

A Prayer

Our prayers always begin with things for which we are thankful, especially those things which we might tend to take for granted. (I am not a great fan of memorized prayers, except for the Lord's Prayer which we pray often.)

When I start the prayer, I just thank God talking to Him with the knowledge that He is sitting there in the room with us, already listening to us, laughing and smiling at our "three things." I'm sure God likes to smile also.

Mary instinctively begins the prayer with the more formal, "Dear Father." I like that too.

Embarrassing Moments

(Beach Towel)

We've all had that experience of "toilet paper stuck on our shoe," or, "toilet paper hanging off the back of our pants." Some have even seen a woman's skirt or dress get caught at the top of her panty hose, exposing what is supposed to be covered. But, I have never heard of the following story happen to anyone else.

Why I Have To Wear Sunglasses
When I Shop At The Walmart In Los Lunas

Had I not been there myself, I would not believe this story to be fact but someone making up the story. However, sadly☺, this is true.

My wife and I stopped at the Walmart in Los Lunas, a quaint town 20 miles south of Albuquerque. When we arrived, I told my wife that I had to run to the bathroom and that I would catch up with her.

As most Walmart stores have one set of bathrooms up front just behind the row of cashiers, I grabbed a grocery cart and wheeled it over to "the bathroom."

When I walked in, I noticed that in the area where there is a row of sinks, there was an elderly lady washing her hands. I assumed that perhaps she was part of a cleaning crew. However, it became apparent that she was a shopper.

I thought to myself, "Should I tell her that she is in the men's room?"

I decided not to embarrass her and so I proceeded to the stalls.

When I got to the room with the stalls, I looked around for a urinal, and finding none, I arrogantly thought to myself, "That figures; the Walmart in Los Lunas doesn't even have all the features that most Walmart stores have."

And so I entered a stall, did my thing and washed my hands before exiting.

As I walked out, I espied, to my horror, a sign indicating that *this was* the ladies room. I quickly picked up my pace but just as I was hurrying out of the bathroom door, three women were headed into the bathroom. When they saw me walk out, they stopped, turned to look at the sign, wondering if they were headed to the wrong room.

I have no idea what they did after that since I hurriedly grabbed my cart, pulled out my sunglasses and walked away as fast as I could.

In my confused little mind, I quickly assessed the various options: (1) Hightail it out of the store? No, someone might call the cops, or, holler out, "Stop that man; he's a pervert!" (2) Get back to my wife as quickly as possible so that everyone could see that I was a nice man shopping with his wife.

I opted for the, "Please, dear wife, make it obvious that I am a normal person, not one of whom one should be afraid ... or have to call the cops."

As I approached my wife, I explained to her what had happened and why I was wearing sunglasses.

She suggested that I take off the sunglasses since they were only making me stand out and instead that I put on a floppy hat she had in her purse.

As Paul Harvey would say, " ... and that ... is the rest of the story."

[Later, as I pondered why I had *not* noticed that this was the ladies restroom, the logical thought hit me, "There was no line going out the door, as most women have to suffer at most public women's restrooms; logically *it had to be* the men's room."]

I Don't Know If You Care Or Not, But ...

My wife and I were vacationing in San Diego, staying at one of the tourist cabins in Pacific Beach. One morning, I decided to walk over to one of the nearby cafes one hundred feet up the boardwalk where half the tourists like me were picking up a "Danish and coffee to go."

There was a bit of a line going from the board-walk up the stairs to the front door. The stairs consisted of a series of "step-ups" where folks stopped to wait until they could start up the next flight of steps as the line moved on again.

As I neared the top steps where there were a few tables with folks enjoying their eats and drinks, I noticed one fellow with a pleasant smile curiously looking at me.

As I neared him, I smiled with a curious look, as in "Do I know you?"

Before I could say anything he grinned even wider, and said, "I don't know if you care or not, but your fly is open."

Baby Blue

Those two embarrassing moments pale in comparison to my "Baby Blue" incident.

The Scene

"They:" gruff highway construction workers who did not really want to be indoors at a six-hour workshop, their deeply tanned faces displaying "Let's get this over with."

"Me:" standing at the front of the room, waiting to begin facilitating the workshop.

The Attire

"They:" Levis which had been laundered many, many times, hanging over scuffed-up work boots.

"Me:" freshly ironed shirt, black dress pants laying over *baby-blue* ladies sandals.

The Mood

"They:" Looking at me with mild amusement.

"Me:" Confidently waiting to explain that I did not typically wear sandals to workshops, especially ladies sandals, *baby-blue* in color.

The Result

"They:" Mild enjoyment at my discomfort, making for a congenial "ice-breaker," after which they saw I was "all business."

"Me:" Mild relief at being "man enough to eat quiche" *and* being able to explain *why* sometimes I might wear ladies baby-blue sandals.

The bottom line: in my haste, I had not double-checked the bag in which I carried my shoes. The workshop was at a location to which my wife and I had been able to drive the day before the workshop. Normally we flew to my workshops and therefore I would have been wearing dress shoes when we left home. Driving to the workshop put me in a less common circumstance where I wore my beat-up old sandals while driving, only to find out an hour before the workshop that I had a choice, my *really* beat up old sandals, or, my wife's new baby blue sandals. It all turned out well, a few of them even congratulating me for my "balanced" sense of humor while making their time worthwhile.

Feel Good Moments

(Hand Towel)

Sometimes, the marvels in this world on which we are tenants are astonishing!

I found several of these marvels in my backyard where I least expected them. They involved several little black ants, a few 1/6-inch cut fingernails, a four-inch twig bridge, a baby bird, a "warm paper towel bowl," and a water-soaked butterfly. These produced some pretty astonishing "Feel Good Moments."

When I'm feeling negative and nothing I do or think helps me feel better, it comforts me to think about "Feel Good Moments" like those. They lift my spirits and reinforce for me that my life has a purpose and that my purpose in life does not have to be earth shattering or headline worthy.

God clarified for me that the purpose of my life was simple, *"Fil, I did not give you the skills and brains of Einstein or Michelangelo, or the writing talents of Hugh Prather or Rod McKuen, or the voice of Celine Dion or Nat King Cole or Andrea Bocelli or Marian Anderson. By the way, I am so sorry that not even the shower helps your voice sound better."* [Note: I added this last sentence because a nun in second grade very sweetly handed me a triangle to play when my second grade class was rehearsing to sing in a school performance. When I took the triangle and continued singing, she again came over to me and quietly said, "No, just play the triangle." Thank you, Sister Donata, for ruining what could have been a marvelous singing career, if only you had encouraged me. ☺]

God continued, *"By the way, I always enjoyed the distinctive sounds you made with your little triangle in second grade. Those rare sounds were as pleasing to me as the exceptional music created by YoYo Ma, Gheorghe Zamfir, Louis Armstrong, Robert Mirabal, and Carlos Nakai."*

"... and in terms of your design skills, I know you wanted to be an architect but I found the creative skills of I M Pei, Felix Candella, and Frank Lloyd Wright pretty amazing. There are so many others who also wanted or needed some guidance, e.g., Neil deGrasse Tyson, Michio Michiokuku, and Chien-Shiung Wu. I believe guiding them was productive, don't you?"

God continued, *"I could go on and on, with more names that you know and so many more that you do not know. My mission for you, Fil, is different, no earthshaking discoveries or productions, yet just as important to the people with whom you share what I have loaned you while you are on this earth ... the ability to make a positive difference in the lives of individuals who need only a little boost. 'Fil, the small booster.' Wear that with love!"*

God continued, *"Remember Kathy the intern in Scottsdale who at the end of the summer gave you a beautiful little book and in it she wrote, 'Thanks, Fil. You'll never know what you did for me.' Well, take it from Me (God), there are a lot more Kathys out there and you'll never know what you did for them. But, trust Me, you made a difference in their lives and not for the sake of your ego, or, to be recognized, but just to be a loving and caring person, to use your cute little 'towels!' To be my messenger! Nothing earth shattering or headline worthy!"*

"And in case you are surprised that I remember you and your little triangle in second grade, remember one of Mary's favorite scriptures: ' ... My thoughts towards you outnumber the grains of sand ...'"
Psalm 139.

Again, some of these "Feel Good Moments" about which I like to remind myself have no front-page news value. They are just encouraging reminders that what we do for the least of God's creatures, we do as God's messengers. (*That* is a great feeling to enjoy every now and then.)

What God Does For Me,
He Allowed Me To Do For One Of His Creatures

A beautiful experience happened to me a few years ago that is still very special for me today. It was such a "Feel Good Moment" that here I am years later still feeling good about what happened.

The morning began in an ordinary fashion. I opened the drapes of our window looking out into our backyard admiring the 35' and 50' tall evergreens we planted 20 years ago when we had our house built. While shaving with my electric razor, I looked around the yard as I always did upon opening the drapes.

As I focused on how much rain had fallen overnight, my gaze was attracted to some slight movement on a green grate about 10 feet from the window. With a slight concern, I noticed that it was one of the wondrous farfalle which fly in and out of our back yard. (I learned from Bart Simpson that *farfalle* is Italian for "butterfly.")

This sort-of-pale-pastel-looking butterfly had apparently been felled by the rain and had not been able to get itself flying again. Due to the rain having soaked its little body, much of the usually visible brilliant colors seemed to have been washed away.

Our little butterfly apparently had been lying in the puddle of water so long that it became water-logged. As a result, it could not move its wings at all, even as the edges of its wings were being eaten by a horde of little black ants. The 20 or 30 little black ants had swarmed its body, apparently first devouring the ends of its wings.

And then God allowed me to do for it what He always does for us. First I picked up the little gal from the wet grate, shook off the ants, and put it on one of our park benches where its wings could dry off. The openings in the seating area of the bench worked well for that.

I then proceeded to fan the little gal in order to help dry off its wings. While that worked some, I surmised that it was too cold for it to not only dry off, but also to warm up.

I therefore moved it to another dry spot -- our protected patio table served that need.

I resumed fanning my new BF with a piece of cardboard from a protein bar box.

The Good Lord then led me to come inside the house and to make a "paper-towel bowl." I took it along with one of my socks and heated them both in the microwave oven.

I then took the warm paper-towel bowl and sock outside. I carefully laid them out, resting them under the cardboard. I moved the butterfly ever so slightly such that one of its wings was exposed to the heat gently rising from the heated sock and bowl.

I repeated that step three times, making sure that the sock especially was warm. This seemed to let the little gal dry off and heat itself as the Good Lord was wont to do.

After about 15 minutes, I gently shook the cardboard upon which the butterfly was laying.

To my delighted surprise, the beautiful little farfalle slowly fluttered away, as though nothing had happened.

And so here I am, very thrilled, and I must admit with a slight tear in my eye, for this unique experience of doing for one of God's little creatures what God does for us countless times a day without our ever being aware of God's "warm-ings."

In addition to thanking God for allowing me the privilege of doing for one of His little creatures what He constantly does for us, I also wondered how many times God has picked me from my puddle of tears or distress, held me warmly in His hands and then opened His hands so that I could fly away and continue with my life. Thank you, God for always loving us unconditionally.

Building Bridges For One Of His Creatures

A couple of other "Feel Good Moments" reminiscent of God taking care of us without our being aware: first – I was watching two little black ants carrying large twigs (large compared to their little bodies, the twigs being three or four times the size of the little fellers).

As I sat on our park bench, I watched one little ant struggle across a 12" x 12" large patio stone. It disappeared when it got to the end of the stone, and then emerged climbing up the adjoining stone. It continued across the next stone and again went down the other side. It repeated the up-and-down journey across two more stones.

I wondered whether they would use "a bridge" if I were to lay some small twigs across the drop from one stone to the other.

Sure enough, the next ant crossed easily using the small twigs and resumed its trek to its ant hole with no problem unaware that "a bridge" had been built for it.

I wonder how many times God has built bridges for me during my life, I being unaware of God's beneficence. Thanks, Big Guy!

Cutting The Burden For One Of His Creatures

On another day, I was at the same park bench, except that this time I was cutting my finger nails.

I watched with surprise that when my finger nails fell to the ground, they were soon picked up by an ant and carried away. Some of the cut nails were quite large for an individual ant and often two or more ants would gather to grab the cut nail together to carry it away. Again, I logically thought that if I were to cut each nail so that it was not so large, that a single ant could carry it by itself. Lo and behold, suddenly there were nine or ten ants each carrying several smaller cut nails.

Once more I wondered how many times God has cut my troubles down to where I could handle them by myself. Thanks again, Lord!

Teaching One Of His Creatures To Fly, With Some Help From Lauren

I will share just one more of these "Feel Good Moments." This one stands out for various reasons. First, my neighbor Lauren, a teenager at the time, was my instructor about what to do. The second thing is that the subject of this "Feel Good Moment" was at the time a nuisance.

The background: a pigeon decided that the perfect place to build its nest was in our cooler up on the roof. Mike, who maintains our swamp cooler, found the nest and pulled it out of the cooler "thingamajiggy," allowing the adult and all the baby pigeons (we thought) to fly away and then tossed the nest to the ground.

As it turned out, there was one young pigeon still in the nest. When the nest landed on the ground, the poor little guy came fearfully out of it. When we tried to catch it, we were unable to surround it.

But then Lauren stepped in. Over the next several days, with her help we were able to get the little guy to practice fluttering its wings as it tried to escape us. We were purposely chasing it so that it fluttered along our side fence. We were also able to maneuver it to the back fence which was much longer in distance giving the young pigeon an opportunity to "fly" further. At the same time, we wanted to make sure the pigeon stayed in the yard until it could truly fly since there were several free-roaming cats in the area.

After several days of "teaching" it to strengthen its wings so that the flutters would produce low-distance flights, the little guy eventually was able to fly up on the roof and after a while fly away.

Again, a lesson from God that we often are given guidance about what to do from unexpected sources. Thank you Lauren; I'm sure the pigeon thanks you also. ☺

Freeing Myself From ...

(Hand Towel)

... Being So Self-Righteous

Every now and then, I feel this tug of regret for what I've said or done.

Why I say or do these things mystifies me since I am fast to complain about others who do or say similar things.

Those who upset me the most are the self-righteous "perfect" human beings.

These have dug at my core since I was 11 or 12 years old, playing with our neighbor's kids in the double driveway adjoining our houses. In the middle of the driveway stood five men chatting, one of them the pastor of a nearby church, the others the organist at another nearby church and two elders from that church.

As I and two of the neighbor's kids were running around the driveway chasing one another, I heard one of the "religious-bigots" say with great certitude that people who were of a certain non-protestant denomination were all going to hell, especially if they were condemned with a certain ethnic sur-name.

Although all of the men were officials in their respective churches, I do not remember anyone disagreeing with him. As I grew older, my anger towards members of that particular denomination grew.

Today, I am particularly incensed when I hear a "so-called Christian" arrogantly speak with a self-righteous "holier than thou" attitude with words meant to denigrate anyone different than they.

As difficult as it is, I am working hard to focus on not letting my anger towards hypocritical self-righteous bigots control me, instead working to "let trust in God control me."

… It's The Principle Of The Thing

Another adage that upsets me is when someone has no argument for the position they are taking, and finally blurts out something like, "It's the Principle of the Thing."

This often occurs when someone is "boxed into a corner" and the person cannot find any reply that explains their opinion or argument.

Politicians often do this with a variation, "the American people deserve to know," or, the media, with "the American people want to know." They do not wish to take ownership, and they have no confidence in their own opinions!

There have been times when hearing, "It's the principle of the thing" did not irritate me because of the discomfort that was evident in the person who was saying it. Instead hearing their last-ditch effort for explaining something the person knew was indefensible, they would blurt out, "It's the principle of the thing." Feeling their discomfort at what they were saying usually elicited a feeling of sympathy for them. I would then say something to help free them from the unnecessary weight they were carrying. This was likely a position that had high-jacked them even though they had no idea why they felt that way, and yet concluded that they needed to defend maintaining that position.

This often happened with my sweet younger sister. She and I came from a somewhat rigid culture, especially the "religion part" of it. (I say "the religion part" as opposed to the "religious part" since "the religion part" is where this "It's the principle of the thing" incubates. It has little to do with being religious as in loving God and respecting one another as God does, "unconditionally." "It's the principle of the thing" is steeped in conditions.)

An example in our culture was that when a woman experienced the death of her spouse, a criterion immediately kicked in that she was "required" to wear black for a year to show that she was in mourning. If the survivor were a widower, not only did the year in mourning kick in, but it also activated a very rigid code of abstaining from any close contact with women.

When my sister observed that our dad had been having lunch or dinner with various females within the "mandatory" 12 months after mom died, my sister became very disturbed. Even when I pointed out that dad had been fully faithful to mom, she persisted with "*but* It's the Principle of the Thing."

I asked her if she could say any of the following was not true: He did not spend money wantonly. He provided. He was always by Mom's side including the last several years of her life when she was non-ambulatory eventually becoming fully bed-ridden.

Even then my sweet little sis carried the burden of "It's the Principle of the Thing" into how she judged my dad. This weight persisted until a few weeks before she died, preceding my father's death. In those last days of her life, with dad present, she was able to experience for herself the kind man her father was.

... Because I Said So

The last "dictum" is what parents or bosses are often guilty of, the rule of "Because I said so."

I was so guilty of this for a long time.

For example, I did not learn to "talk with" my children while they were "youngens." I recall several times coming home from a long day at work, only to be greeted by my wife with, "you've got to talk to ... " or "you've got to spank ...."

I do not recall ever asking what they had done or sitting down with them to talk about what had happened. The fact that their mother wanted me to discipline them was all that was necessary. In this case it was "Because your mother said so."

Too late to have learned to talk with my own children, I did learn to "talk with" my new wife's daughter. Soon after we were married, there was a situation where I was disciplining her much in the same way as I had done with my children.

Her mother pulled me aside and said. "I appreciate you caring for her enough to discipline her, but I usually explain to her what she did wrong." Hmm, I thought to myself, "what a great idea."

Again fortunately I am sometimes a fast learner and in this case, I soon found myself asking HB *why* she had done what she did. It was not a Dr. Spock approach; it was respecting this little nine-year old so that I could understand what it was that motivated her to do what she had done.

I never again had to "discipline" HB. We developed a mutually unconditional respect for one another. Would that I had learned that type of respect with my own children. I'm sorry, kids.

I was also guilty of using "Because I said so" when I first became "the boss."

OMG, I cannot believe how inane I was. The first time I *was the boss*, I would purposely stand at the front door of the office so that anyone who was late would know that I saw that they were late. What an idiot!

Fortunately, I learned fast, which was a good thing since I made every mistake a manager can make in my first three months as "the boss." Finally one person who felt he should have gotten the promotion and not I (an outsider) caught me just as we were closing up at 5:00 p.m. on a Friday. He was not trying to be helpful as he fully dissected me with his biting comments about how I was bringing the office to a stop; *that* got my attention.

One of the supercilious actions I had been taking was to insist on "proofing" everything that the staff produced before being sent out. What an ignoramus I was!

That weekend I went into the office on Saturday and again on Sunday and put everything back on the desks of everyone who was waiting for my "approval" along with an apology.

I am proud to say that after that major fiasco, we moved ahead even more efficiently than under their previous boss. Many projects that had taken years to complete, we got done in less than a year.

The staff began bringing to my attention other things that they thought could be improved if we took care of things ourselves instead of hiring consultants. And we did that! That was one of the main reasons why we were able to cut the time in completing projects by months.

Never did I make myself a fool again by thinking that being "the boss" somehow gave me enhanced knowledge or unrivalled powers. After that, I saw what every good manager should see *unconditionally,* that everyone has an important role, mine was to see that the necessary resources were available and to act as the background support for anything the team needed. Interestingly, this progress made me even more the *valid definition* of what "A boss is."

"I'm Sorry Kids!"

(Bath Towel)

Note: One of my best friends shared with me why he was emotionally overwrought about the chasm between him and his children after his divorce. He sincerely hoped to spare others from the pain he and his children have endured separately for a long time, each feeling abandoned by the other. I agreed to tell his story in my book since I support his goal in sparing others from this avoidable pain.

This chapter is offered in the *first person* tense. Here is *his* story:

"This is something which I share reluctantly. However, if even one person understands the deep emotions involved in a story like this, it will have been worthwhile. The value will be heightened if anyone decides, after reading this, to contact an estranged parent who for the wrong reason became separated from the children. Hoping for that result ameliorates some of the pain which I have carried for the last ten–plus years.

Divorce is the foundation of this painful episode; however, what often happens after the divorce is even more painful. (A well-known and very successful celebrity was quoted in an issue of *Parade Magazine* saying, "The hardest and most painful thing that's ever happened to me in my life was divorce." Success apparently does not ameliorate the agony. The grief is deep and often unsurmountable, and unbelievably, it *can* be made worse.)

On a recent episode of 'God Friended Me,' Jacob, a young man, is looking for his estranged father.

It turns out that Jacob's mother did not want Jacob's father around after she discovered that she was pregnant. Years later, 'the child,' 17 years old at this point, tracks down his father and questions him about why he abandoned him and his mother.

Even after Jacob hears that his maternal grandfather forcefully demanded that Jacob's father, his mother's boyfriend at the time, go away and never again have contact with his mother, Jacob could not understand how his father could have **left him.**

His father tearfully tells Jacob, 'I didn't want to leave you, but it was very clear that I was not going to be allowed to have any part in your life. And so I left.'

After several hours of back-and-forth accusations, explanations, and more questions, Jacob shrugs his shoulders trying to understand how that could have happened. He continues to refuse to accept any explanation about why his father left his mother.

More importantly, Jacob refuses to accept any valid reason why his father *left him.*

After a few minutes of silently looking at the ground with tears streaming down his cheeks, running past his chin and finally dropping teardrop by teardrop to the sidewalk, Jacob slowly walks away, leaving his father staring down at the pavement.

After taking several steps, Jacob turns around and sees his father still standing silently, now looking up at Jacob, with tears also running down his face.

Jacob stops, looks straight at his estranged father and angrily hollers,

'YOU *left* me! .... You *left* ME!'

And this brings me to my 'own children,' now in their 30s and 40s. I have been estranged from three of them for more than 10 years through several birthdays and Father's Days.

When my oldest sister died, one of my daughters became angry with me because I had taken issue with my sister's husband who had sent out an insulting email shortly after my sister's death.

The email described the opposite of what my wife and I had actually done during my sister's last weeks. The fact was that my wife and I had travelled to be with my sister after learning that she had been diagnosed with pancreatic cancer and had only six to eight weeks to live.

We spent an extremely loving week with her and her family. To help ease the pressure on the family, we either took meals to them every day or if they preferred, went to a restaurant with whomever wished to go out to eat.

Intermittently we visited with my sister who had confided in me before we arrived that she got tired very easily and preferred visitors to stay only 15-20 minutes at a time, and importantly, not to invite themselves to stay for dinner (as one group of visiting family members had done). Although she had a hospital bed in their master bedroom, she could hear the sometimes boisterous laughter from the living room, even with the door closed.

With that in mind, my wife and I went on this trip prepared to work out of our hotel room, having scheduled our work such that we could do work from our temporary office. This necessitated taking our laptop and work files from home to make our efforts productive.

This worked out well allowing me to have time every day for a week with my sister, as well as with her family.

The time I spent with my sister was one of the most tender times she and I had ever spent together. We talked about everything other than her cancer, unless she wanted to share that she needed another self-administered 'shot' of morphine because the pain had become unbearable.

There were only two other times when she and I had enjoyed as deep a loving sister-brother visit. One of these times was when she spent a week with me after her husband had unexpectedly told her that he wanted a divorce because he was seeing someone else.

After my sister's death, my then brother-in-law unexpectedly sent an email to all those we mutually knew. The email was full of lies and disdain for me and my wife. Having known him for more than 30 years, I knew what kind of a snake he was and therefore had taken his latest diatribe in stride, but I could not get over how the lies hurt my wife.

When I said something to my daughter, she became angry with me for some still-to-this-date unknown reason, presumably I was supposed to support and forgive him. (She was unaware of his unfaithfulness and other abuses that he laughingly promulgated all his life. If one only knew him for hours at a time, he could be quite charming.)

Shortly after his email, my previously extra-loving daughter apparently talked two of her siblings into somehow believing that the caring father I had been was a lie.

After hearing Jacob's point of reference, I better understand how vulnerable my kids were when their mother and I divorced; in their two-to-eight-year old minds, I had left them. The thought that I had left them was repeated ad nauseum by their mother, even though she had caused the breakdown in our marriage by having a child with another man.

For the sake of the kids, I wish I could have found a way to actually save the marriage even after her unfaithfulness. We went to several marriage counselors, all of whom she refused to go back to after one or two sessions. Her excuse, 'They always take your side.' This was her response to all of them, male or female, even though they were counselors who she herself had selected.

My kids were also unaware that at the time of our divorce, I asked my attorney to check with a judge to determine what chance I had in petitioning the court for custody of the kids, at least custody of my daughters. The judge's response sickened me; I would have to gather evidence to prove my wife as an unfit mother. Even though I was angry at my wife for having a child with another man, there was no way that I would color her as unfit to the detestable extent the judge indicated I would have to do in order to demonstrate her as 'unfit' in order to have a chance of gaining custody. Even then, I was told it would be a 50-50 chance that custody would not go to the mother.

As time went by, she continued to remind the kids that it was *I who had left them*.

A few years ago (over 20 years after the divorce), I found out that not only had their mother cheated on me but that she had lied to them telling them that I was not sending her any money for their care.

In addition to the monthly child support and alimony I sent her, she often "borrowed" money from me totaling a rather large sum (over $135,000 in 2020 value). Furthermore, she apparently had also been pilfering the gifts, cards, and money that I had been sending the kids for their birthdays, Christmas, special occasions, and 'just because.' As far as they were aware, I had been ignoring all these special occasions.

This along with their not knowing that I had worked to get legal custody of them would understandably not soften the hurt with which they have lived ever since. Even though she lied and stole from them, *she was there* and *I was not*.

For years, I believed that they wanted to have nothing to do with me since they were not even acknowledging the gifts, cards and money I was sending them directly.

After sending them stamped, self-addressed envelopes so they could just stick in their notes and leave them for the mail carrier to pick up and deliver to me, and receiving nothing in return, I retreated into a cave of 'I should not bother them anymore.'

Yet I could not give up that easily and I embarrassingly even resorted to sending them paper placemats. I asked them to put those placemats under their plates when they ate their meals and then stick them into the large stamped self-addressed envelopes so that I could at least "feel" them even if it was just in my mind. I found out decades later that they were never aware of any of that effort. Just as well, this was a rather pathetic description of my already unsteady mental state regarding the kids.

Too late, I found out why they never acknowledged the cards and gifts; they never received any of them.

With the repeated 'reminders' that their mother was present and I was not, it is understandable that they might think, *'We had nothing to do with our mother having a child with another man while married to you. We're sorry that mom cheated on you, and that she lied to you and that she lied to us, but even if we could understand what she did to you, the fact is that YOU LEFT US!'"*

[The following note is from my friend who shared this story *and* from me:

Note To Estranged Parents and Children: Be sure that the *reason* for your estrangement is a *valid* one.]

Lessons Learned, Five Of Them

(Hand Towel)

We all learn lessons throughout our lives, no matter our age. A toddler learns; a senior citizen learns.

Unfortunately, I am sometimes a bit slow on the "up-take" and instead of learning a lesson because of what I have done wrong, I look for someone else to take the blame, "*I* couldn't have screwed that up!" At times, it seems more gratifying to be stubborn and/or arrogant in ignoring them as lessons learned, "Let's just forget about it."

I am a bit embarrassed to mention some of the lessons I have learned; however, I do find the last one amusing. ☺

In All Things Give Thanks,
For This Is The Will Of God Concerning You

This scripture comes from 1 Thessalonians 5:18: "In all things give thanks, for this is the will of God concerning you."

My wife shared this scripture with me about seven years into our marriage. The Good Lord gave her a deep faith in the Bible which sustained her through some very rough years. My appreciation of the Bible is that it helped my beautiful, wonderful, generous wife survive until we became one.

As it turns out, this particular "Word of God" also has helped me through some rough times.

There are times, however, when what happens is so devastating that I ask God, "Are you kidding me? You want me to give You thanks for this crap that just happened?" (God being unconditionally patient did not strike me when I said that word. Fortunately, God had much more patience with me than what I had with what had just happened.)

In the process of learning to trust and believe these words, "Give thanks!" I must confess that sometimes I just *give in* with a reluctant, "Okay God, I give you thanks for this rotten experience; now what?"

(Actually I didn't really believe that I could fully trust God the first few times. However, after several "Okay, I'll give it a try," I am a firm believer that thanking God for *all* things "because it is His will" works no matter how preposterous the circumstance. By the way, that is "in *all* things.")

This Is What I Heard You Say

This lesson is mine: I noticed that folks get into the silliest of arguments when one person says to the other, "... but that's not what you said."

I learned that when I said, "This is what I heard you say," it eliminated the opening for an argument; the other person could not argue with what I heard.

It also congenially opened the door for clarification, "What *did* you say?"

Additionally, I am being polite and respectful, acknowledging that what I heard *may not be* what the other person actually said (or often) what they meant to say.

This has been a simple lesson but a very effective one.

For A Happy Marriage, "I'm Sorry For My Part"

This lesson is also mine: For a happy marriage, and for any happy relationship, it helps to say after any "argument," "I'm Sorry For My Part."

This easy statement erases any need to continue the spat, or to pinpoint "the culprit."

It does not lay or take blame.

It moves beyond the need to find fault, focusing on moving on; who can argue with that as a desirable solution? ☺

Who/What Angers Me Controls Me

I don't recall where I first heard this lesson, "Who/What Angers Me Controls Me." Over the years, I have often written down thoughts and ideas which spoke to me. Sometimes I have taken some of those words of wisdom and tailored them so that they would mean something specific to me. So please pardon me when I do not attribute credit to the original author.

What I do know is that whenever I ignored this lesson, I stupidly spent a great deal of energy thinking about being wronged and plotting how I could exact revenge. If seriously aggrieved, my revenge had to be of a "sufficient" level of retribution. (What a relief when I realized that I help myself best by just "labeling" that person with a really nasty name even if it was just an imagined put-down in my mind. Enjoying that thought released the control which that anger had on me.)

It also reminded me that "One can tell how big a person is by what it takes to discourage them, because that is what controls them."

The time is better spent by acknowledging that what I should focus on are the words, "Let Trust In God Control Me."

Head Drop!

My wife and I developed this lesson in a way that surprised us both. We noticed that one of us (usually me) sometimes babbled on and on with the other person no longer really listening. If listening, the person was "listening" just to be polite, certainly not due to any true interest in what the other was expounding.

One day, one of us did a "Head Drop" as the other was going on and on about who-knows-what. (A Head Drop is the simple movement of the head as it drops onto one's shoulder.)

This sort-of-politely conveyed that the "Head Dropper" was no longer interested in what was being said and was ready to move on to the next topic.

We decided that this "lesson" was a much more valuable way to say, "Okay, I'm ready to move on." This is certainly much more civil than declaring, "No one is listening to you!" or, "Will you just shut up!" ☺

We also found that sometimes the "babbler" was so carried away with "his" babbling that, having lost eye contact with "his audience," he was unaware that a "Head Drop" had just been "awarded." In this case, it became necessary to also softly holler out "Head Drop!"

Living In My Failures

(Bath Towel)

Note: This chapter is proving to be the most re-visited chapter in that I continue to add to it due to recurring bouts of *actually* "Living In My Failures." For me, "Living In My Failures" is an omnipresent feeling, sometimes under the surface (in my subconscious) but always there.

After reading this draft several times in order to see whether it makes sense, I have found reading it to be exhausting. The material in these "Bath Towel" chapters is pretty heavy stuff. I have found that it is a good idea to take a break when reading these chapters, maybe doing some grazing in chapters where there is a light content, e.g., "Embarrassing Moments," "Brief Encounters," or, "Feel Good Moments." (Many of these light chapters are composed of very short stories; "Brief Encounters" has 11 short stories, "Feel Good Moments" has four short stories.)

Today I am dealing with the loss of ease of mobility reinforced by a severe leg pain. Even when I stand, the pain is an "11" on a scale of "0 to 10." This has totally taken over my life and affected how I view just about everything. For instance, I cussed uncontrollably a few minutes ago when I *almost* tipped over my cup of coffee. The fact that it was not even remotely close to tipping was irrelevant. In my cloud of anger, the fact that I *almost* tipped it said to me that I was a klutz. "Only a klutz would be so uncoordinated!" *After all, it could have tipped.* Wow! "Living In My Failures!"

The fact is that when I am "Living In My Failures" it is almost impossible to accept anything as successful unless it is perfect. In the world of "Living In My Failures," there is no such thing as real "success." Nothing is ever good enough; there is always something that can be made better.

This pain in my leg which has necessitated my use of crutches to sit, stand, and walk around (even if only temporarily), causes me to react as though it is a permanent change in my life.

Continuing to live in my failures, I then punish myself for being so selfish when I think of the countless veterans who are walking permanently with crutches, or with prosthetics. [Note added during the Covid-19 pandemic: As of today, well over half a million Americans have died in the past 12 months. Here I sit healthy, having received all my vaccinations, while over two million family members and friends are suffering unbearable pain due to the losses of their loved ones who are no longer here to share their love, life, and laughter. How dare I complain about *almost* tipping over my coffee cup!]

How Can I Accept A Compliment If My Work Is Not Perfect?

My wife, who describes herself as a "recovering perfectionist" dropped this thought on me, "How can I accept a compliment if my work is not perfect?"

I had never considered that thought as my point of reference, but it certainly explains my rage when I *almost* tip over a cup of coffee. "Only a klutz would be so uncoordinated! Only someone who is not perfect would tip over a cup." And although I did not actually tip the cup over, I was *close enough* to tipping it, thus demonstrating that I am not perfect. (Boy, talk about Ego!)

(In a recent episode of "Blue Bloods," Danny Reagan is talking with his brother, Jamie Reagan, who had earlier talked "a jumper" out of diving off a New York City bridge. After being talked off the bridge, the young man sought out his girlfriend who had broken up with him precipitating his suicidal depression. When "the jumper" finds the girl friend, he kills her. Danny tells Jamie that a police officer's job is not always easy or perfect. He asks Jamie if that was his first experience with "a jumper." Then Jamie asks Danny the same question. Danny becomes visibly upset

89

replying that he has dealt with several jumpers including one who after hours of being talked to by Danny finally jumped. Danny's last words are, "There isn't a night when I'm going to bed that I don't see his face as he turned and jumped." The one he could not save is the one he remembers; he does not recall the numerous ones whose lives he did save.)

One exercise I frequently did when conducting workshops was to ask the class participants to share 99 compliments about people with whom they had worked over the years. Then, I asked them to share one criticism about someone with whom they had worked.

I then asked, "In a week, what are you going to remember, the 99 compliments or the one criticism?"

Not a single person in any of the classes ever said they would remember the compliments.

The negatives and the criticisms stand out for most of us.

It is *so* easy to continue to put ourselves down. Souls on the verge of suicidal depression are fully immersed in this unrealistic, negative reality. For many, that is the story of their lives, often reinforced by teachers, parents and preachers. It is no surprise that this pushes an already vulnerable person towards suicide.

Depressions, One after Another

When I began writing this chapter many months ago, I was fighting one of the five worst depressions in my life, on the level of suicidal depression.

At that time, I took *The Shack* to read out in my backyard, mostly because of the part where Mack says to Jesus, "Jesus, I feel so lost." Jesus responds, "I know, Mack, but it is not true. I am with you, and I am not lost ... therefore, you are not lost."

As I sat on one of our park benches, I thought to myself, "Sorry, Jesus, I don't know where you are. Therefore you can't help me."

At that moment, one of Max Lucado's wonderful messages came to mind. In this message, Max tells about a time when he was feeling lost and his wife asked him what was going on. When he finished telling her, she pointed out to him that in all his description of what was going on, he did not mention God once. "Where is God in all of this?" she asked him.

Since hearing that message, I ask myself when dealing with my "lost-nesses," "Where is God in all this, Fil?"

As I continued to sit on the bench, after telling God that I did not know where He was and therefore He could not really help me, He pointed my eyes towards the foot of the bench. Laying there was an odd, egg-shaped stone about two inches long and 1 ½ inches wide. The stone was mostly charcoal gray, but it also had large speckles of cloud-white flecks interspersed among the gray core.

As I picked up the stone and studied it, I felt that God was saying to me, "Take this Fil as a reminder that when you are living in your failures, you are living in the gray. How different does the stone look when you focus on the white instead of focusing on the gray? Does it look any different?"

The more I looked at the cloud-white flecks, they seemed to become snow-white in color. As the white stood out, the gray went more into the background. After a few minutes, I barely noticed the gray.

The message I recognized was, "Live in your successes; focus on the white part of the stone. If you live in your failures, you will certainly be lost because the gray will become all encompassing; there will be *no* white."

I still have a lot of work to do about figuring out who I am today.

Let Trust In God Control Me

Fortunately, God has helped me to understand that a better option to "What angers me, controls me" is to choose a better control, "Let trust in God control me."

However, to "Let trust in God control me" has not been easy. (Currently, fires are raging in the West; floods and winds are making millions of people homeless on the east side of our country. We and the rest of the world are also dealing with the Covid-19 pandemic plus political struggles, starvation, massive chaos in leadership.) It is *so* easy to let anger control me, or to let politics control me.

Apparently, I am not alone in these destructive thoughts that too often control me. Doctors and other professionals report abnormal rises in anxiety and depression. Nonetheless, just because others are allowing these failures to control them does not mean that I must follow that path. If anything, it is even more important that I focus on letting trust in God control me.

Mercifully when I awoke this morning, I realized that letting "trust in God control me" has kept me on a positive path of knowing that God is there for me, for my wife, and for all others. As difficult as it is to believe these facts, God **is** here, all around us.

Also important is being aware that expectations rule. When I "let trust in God control me," my expectations are real. Having to use crutches would have been a catastrophic failure a while back. Now with trust in God as the "control," it allows me to realize that just because I am not able to do something that I want to do, does not mean that I am a failure. I remind myself what Mack realizes (in *The Shack*) " ... that crashing wasn't painful at all, but only a slow-motion bounce."

My last thought for now regarding "Living In My Failures" is being aware that failure is relative. What failure is for one person may be success for another.

Phew, this is exhausting.

More Depressions ... Here We Go Again

Here I go again, several weeks after the depressions I mentioned above. Today's depression is even worse than those. Nothing seems to be working: my laptop went blank; the toilet keeps running, and no one can come out for 36 hours; it's gonna be an expensive water bill.

This follows on the heels of another deep depression a few days ago. That one came out of nowhere; while watching a TV show, a male actor said, "I know I can do better." Immediately I had the following thought, "I know *I* can do better." That was quickly erased by the following thoughts: "I have no idea how to do that." "I have nothing to offer." "This book is a waste of time."

Immediately, I was transported to the world of "living in *my own failures,*" no stops necessary to pick up any luggage – living in my head rent-free was all the excess baggage I needed for this journey! *I've got enough extra valises, handbags, brief cases, and any other form of luggage a person might need, enough for a whole bunch of other folks. Come on, people, join me!* **Please don't.** (One truth on which we can all agree is that misery *does* indeed love company.)

The frightening realization is that living in my own failures stops me from living in any successes. I was unable to shake off that feeling for over two days.

Living In My Goodness, Living In My Successes; Maybe It Will Work This Time

After two days and still in the midst of this trauma, something surprising and amazing happened. This time it was something good: God gently suggested that I put "the problems" into perspective; "look at the cloud-white flecks on the stone; think about what is going well."

I asked myself, "Have any of *my* problems been life or death issues? How do they compare with hurricane Isaias and the thousands of homes and businesses damaged beyond use at the same time as the Covid-19 pandemic rages? How do they compare to the thousands of heroes suffering from the effects of war? How about the countless young and elderly souls feeling lonely and not appreciated? How about the healthcare workers being heroes every day to help heal the rest of us ... even the irresponsible ones who need their help because they chose not to wear masks or get vaccinated during the pandemic? How about the police and fire fighters who respond whenever any of us calls 911 asking for their help? Comparatively speaking, I have nothing about which to complain; in fact, I have innumerable blessings to appreciate."

Living In My Failures, Real And Imagined

Delightful Pastor Rick Warren in his wonderful book, *The Purpose Driven Life*, explains that "everyone lives at one of three levels: survival, success, or significance."

He goes on to say, "Most of the world lives at the survival level. Half of the world's six billion people live on less than two dollars a day. Over one billion live on less than one dollar a day. That's the survival level."

"If you live in the United States, you live at the success level, even if you feel poor. Most of the world would love to have our problems."

He continues, "You were made for far more than success. You were created for significance."

I have no argument that we "were made for far more than success" and that we "were created for significance." I wish that I found it that simple, however. The fact is that many "successful people" do not succeed at even "surviving" although they live in the United States and have more "dollars" than they can spend; yet *failure* still controls their lives. Think of all the celebrities who have taken their lives.

Would that these three levels were my reality. I must work harder to remember the truth that I was "made for far more than success" and that I was "created for significance."

I often ask myself why I get so upset about things, mostly the small things, like an American Airlines customer service agent not picking up my call. What I was mostly wrestling with was that the recording continued to ask ad nauseum questions "in order to better serve you." I started screaming at the recording. All I managed to accomplish was to upset my wife. The AA guy never heard anything I said since I was still on hold.

So then I hung up and called again. Amazingly it worked; I was no longer on hold, but then I had to talk with someone who turned out to be rather unsympathetic to my reason for calling. I again became and remained upset. It was too late to understand that this was not *my* failure ...

                    ... but why let a good failure go to waste!?

Overheard on the movie set in my mind, **Rehearsing My Failures**:

"Scene 81, Take 14 ... Failure"

"Okay, let's repeat that!" ... (me tipping my cup).

"Oops, hey! The blankety-blank cup *did not tip* again!"

"Let's try that again!"

"Scene 81, Take 15 ... Failure"

"... and let's get it **wrong** this time!"

You Underestimate Yourself

Fortunately, after several "lost days," totally wasted in terms of accomplishments, or, even producing simple results, something moved me to at least clean out an old shelf with a stack of papers.

This project looked like something that I could handle. Basically it was going through outdated papers which were no longer relevant.

As I began to toss out two sets of stapled papers, I came across a copy of one of Pastor Skip Heitzig's messages. Highlighted at the bottom of the first page were the words, "Every morning ... spend your mornings with God in prayer and ... receive whatever you'll need for the day."

Paper-clipped to these was a copy of a poem I had sent to my mother-in-law a year ago when she was talking about wanting to join her husband who had died 20+ years earlier. Highlighted on that sheet of paper were the words, "There is work still waiting for you ... You must not idly stand by; do it now – while life remaineth."

I Tire, Time To Take A Break

Writing and reading this is exhausting. I believe it is time to take a break. I will graze with one of the three short stories in "Embarrassing Moments," or, with one of the 11 short stories in "Brief Encounters." Those chapters make me smile even though I wrote them a long time ago and have re-read them many times. Reading them *is* living in my successes.

Maybe Some Solutions

"It works better when we do it together," Jesus tells Mack in *The Shack.*

Let trust in God control me.

In all things give thanks for this is the will of God concerning you (1Thess.5:18)

Sometimes, the pain does not go away; you have to grow around it.

Remember: God's love is always with us; pass it on!

Always walk with A Rose Bowl Of Love, with A Rose Bowl Of Patience, and with A Rose Bowl Of Trust In God.

Follow my Mary's advice: when a plan goes awry, consider the change as an adventure. "We're on an adventure" immediately lifts me away from "the failure." Being on an adventure turns the negative experience into an energizing exploration.

Something happened in the last few days that I am very hopeful will assist me in escaping from the world of "living in my failures." First, instead of cussing and going into a rage, I sing "Red Light!"

Here is my "Red Light" story:

When driving to my Covid-19 vaccination site, I had to stop at *all* the traffic signals because they were *all* red ... thoroughly frustrating me. As a result of these delays, however, I ended up in line next to a wonderful young nurse named Stephanie. During the 40-minute wait in line, Stephanie and I struck up a conversation that included me telling her about my book. Her genuine interest in what I told her about the book reinforced for me that what I was writing was important to finish.

Had I not run into every red light from my home to the vaccination site, I would not have met Stephanie, told her about the book, shared a few pages with her, and received a critical reinforcement that I should continue to work on this book.

Hence, "Red light!" reminds me that *the failure* about which I am getting upset is happening for a very good reason.

As God reminds us: "In All Things Give Thanks, For This Is The Will Of God Concerning You," 1 Thessalonians 5:18

"Lucidity"

(Hand Towel)

The word "lucidity" is a seldom used word, but one that is appropriate for describing a unique vision that I experienced. Initially, I chose not to look up the word in the dictionary because I wanted a word that *was mine* to tell *my* story in as clear a way as possible recognizing that the full story is quite complex and not at all easy to follow. Making it *my word* assured me that the clarification I wished to share satisfied *my criteria.*

I started with the word "lucid" from the Latin meaning "seeing clearly, easy to understand," and added the very useful suffix "-ity" which seems to magically elevate the credibility of just about any topic to the stature of being a fact. [That "credibility" reinforced my little game of satisfying my criteria, irrespective of how it "played" out in the world. Admittedly, a little weird, but "I never promised you a rose garden." ☺]

In *this* case, "lucidity" is a word that best describes "a series of singular events which when coupled with another series of events makes the first series of events "make sense." During my vision, this coupling of events was repeated countless times, resulting in my being able to see more clearly all the occurrences that lead to Mary and me coming together 20 some years after we first met.

In this context, things that occurred earlier *in each of our lives* played a distinctive role in connecting several events which happened in each of our lives over the course of several years. (If this is confusing, just go with "being at the right place at the right time.")

"Lucidity" has helped me put into perspective the experiences of the past, both positive and negative, and to reinforce God's reminder that "I always answer your prayers, not all the time as you believe to be the best way and certainly not on your imprecise time table."

This concept of what I call "lucidity" was born in my little head one summer day when my wife and I had been working hard to create an attractive back yard for our recently built house.

My wife, being the trooper that she is, works until she is ready to drop. This happened that day when she suddenly declared the work we were doing on the side of the house was "enough for now." (I learned early in our marriage that when we jointly work on a project, it is best that one of us be "the decider-bee" and the other be "the worker-bee.")

This day, I was the worker-bee. So when she firmly pronounced our work for the day completed " *è finito*!" no questions were asked.

The dictum of *no mas* was reinforced right after she asked me to bring her the patio lounge chair so that she could sit down and rest. I decided to join her and also brought out a patio chair which I put down next to her lounge chair.

Mary having disappeared into the house, I waited for 15-20 minutes and when it became apparent that she had no intention of coming back out to sit in the requested chair, I approached our back patio door, and being a bit dusty from the work, chose to call out to her, "Are you coming back out?"

Her brief response was "No, I've changed my mind."

Although she had called it "a day," I stayed to ponder what to do next. Looking back at the chairs, I decided that I would sit out there nonetheless, since she sometimes changed her mind more than once.

In addition, I hoped that she would come back out so we could perform our celebratory walk. [When we accomplished anything of which either or both of us were proud, we *youthfully* performed an *admiration tour*, complimenting ourselves or the person who had done "a good jobbie" (as she recalls her father telling her when she was two or three years old and had done a good job).]

At that point, I did a celebration tour inside my head and instead decided to sit out in the patio chair by myself.

After about five minutes, I decided I wanted something to drink, perhaps a nice glass of cold ginger ale and something to munch on.

So I walked over to the back door but, being acutely aware that I was *persona non grata* inside the house while still wearing the dirty work clothes, I merely opened the back door and called, "Mary, would you get me some ginger ale and some crackers?"

When she failed to acknowledge my multiple requests, I said to myself, "Screw it; I'm going inside anyway, and I'm going to let old Jim Beam take a little swim in the ginger ale and I'm going to enjoy some cheese with the crackers."

Being content with my decisions, I went back out and sat in the patio chair which was facing into the north-east corner of our large backyard. It was still somewhat of a bare area, sans landscaping save for three 24-inch tall tomato plants.

While savoring "my ginger ale," I closed my eyes and experienced one of the most remarkable visions in my life. Although everything was dark, I could yet "sense" light.

As I studiously looked closer, the foreground began to blend with the background; my vision became reminiscent of a darkened movie theater.

As I looked closer into that blankness, I "saw" two lines of travel moving against the dark background. Each line of travel seemed to be traveling on a one-lane road.

One line in particular appeared to be a flashback into my life. The other line appeared to be the path of travel in Mary's life.

Every now and then, little lights would blink as they traveled along the "veins of travel," starkly contrasted against the darkness.

I experienced more and more flashes of light as each line moved along individual paths. Each time the lights flashed, memories of events from the past "came into view" even though the episodes had occurred 30-40 years earlier.

Each time I remembered these events, they mysteriously gave clarity to why they had happened; my life seemed to make sense, blending the good memories and the bad memories.

Remarkably, the blends of good and bad memories produced an understanding of why bad things had happened, things which were in no way answers to my prayers. Amazingly, it made sense that God had indeed answered my prayers but not in the way nor on the time table that I had sought.

Highlights of Mary's life also made sense. At certain points along those lines our paths intersected and there would be more vibrant "pops" of light. These mini-explosions of intensity included the time when Mary and I first met in Kansas 40 years earlier. They also included the regeneration of our friendship which happened 10 years after we first met. This renewed relationship rose to a level more pleasant than merely exchanging birthday cards from hundreds of miles away. Now we were each living in southern California, I in San Diego, she in Los Angeles.

As the vision continued, I pieced together the various individual parts of our lives, the positive *and* the negative. Now, there seemed to be more compelling reasons for *some of the lights*, better clarifying the question, "Why, God?"

After a few minutes, those little lights and the routes on which they traveled turned into a vision of the full pathways of travel through which my life had undergone. I also saw blurry lines, going back decades, where Mary's life had taken her.

The final intersection of our lives was due to several, separate, very dark situations in each of our lives.

This is in fact a very complex and long story. The bottom line is that, had many things not happened, including the darkest times in each of our lives, we would not likely have come together for the remainder of our lives as we have. Some of what happened in our individual travels were experiences that no one should ever have to suffer. Yet, had these nightmares not happened, our paths would not have come together unless God had other plans to bring us together.

This series of experiences is a clear testament to God's message, "In all things, give thanks, for this is the will of God concerning you."
1 Thessalonians 5-18

This has helped me see the past more clearly. The question of " *Why* did this happen to me?" becomes irrelevant. What seemed like clearly bad incidents ultimately led to truly great results.

Looking back, the three best experiences in my life came about due to three extraordinary heartbreaks. The first of these "best experiences" was Mary and I coming together as one. The other two experiences were the best professional achievements in my life, each the result of an earlier traumatic professional failure.

Miracles

(Hand Towel)

For a long time, I did not believe in miracles. And then, experiences in my life would not let me ignore them.

Let me share a few truly memorable ones; these are pretty cool.

The Sixth Level

One miracle occurred while I was struggling to dig a 15-foot long, crescent shaped, *flat* trench upon which to place 4" x 12" tan retainer-wall blocks. This trench would define the planter we were building along the back wall of our yard and thus *had* to be perfectly horizontal.

After several hours of adjusting and re-adjusting several carpenter levels, I smiled at my efforts to create a trench where the bricks would lay perfectly flat, including the area around the two curves in the planter. To achieve this even alignment, I was using six carpenter levels.

As I stood up, I was very proud that I had conquered aligning the sixth carpenter level in order to produce a complete end-to-end alignment where I had all the bubbles *near* the middle, meaning that the trench was close to being perfectly flat. Close enough! ☺

Unexpectedly I felt *a tap* on my shoulder and a voice pleasantly asked, "What does water do?" Then I realized that it must be Jesus just standing there smiling at all my levels and thinking, "These humans, aren't they a kick! If they can make it complicated they will not hesitate to do so."

In response to the question, "What does water do?" I smilingly removed all six levels, poured water into the trench and waited to see if the water flowed in any direction. If it flowed, the trench was not flat. When the water simply "puddled," my trench *was* flat.

Jesus being a carpenter, I was a bit hurt that He did not acknowledge that I had used six carpenter levels. But no, He had to embarrass me with, "What does water do?" ☺

No matter whether I did it in a simple way or a complicated way, the wall is still perfectly flat 19 years later. (I just took a level today to check it and I was able to verify that the bubbles are still "close enough" to the middle ☺.)

(If one wishes to argue that this was not a miracle, I dare you to align six carpenter levels end-to-end in order to achieve a horizontally aligned trench, especially going around two curves. The *tap* on my shoulder was so real that I turned around to look to see *who* was there. Miracle? You bet! Not a biggie, but then most of God's miracles are so routine we seldom notice, like those pesky hydrogen and oxygen molecules coming together to make water. ☺)

The Hands

One miracle with which there is no argument is one where Mary and I were both eyewitnesses. To describe all the details would result in a novella. Therefore, I will only tell the highlights.

One September 17th, in order to celebrate one of Mary's special birthdays, I made a reservation at what was at the time my favorite bed and breakfast inn, the Hacienda de Chimayo, located in the very quaint village of Chimayo, about 25 miles north of Santa Fe. My favorite room is *Siete,* overlooking the grove of trees across the two lane road.

The room was uniquely charming, with a wood burning fireplace and a pleasantly quiet courtyard with several small fruit trees outside the front door. A quaint white wooden balcony overlooked the quiet two lane rural road and the wooded meadow across the road where one could often find horses grazing.

After we had unloaded our luggage, we walked across the road to the *Restaurante de Chimayo*, another uniquely picturesque eating place, creatively tiered up the hillside on which it sits.

After a pleasant dinner, we returned to our room where Mary opened the birthday cards and gifts I had brought.

The next morning, September 18th, after a delightful and appealing breakfast, we drove down the mile to the *Santuario de Chimayo*, a church which was built in 1816; it is now a National Historical Landmark.

After arriving at the Church, we lit some candles, and then I went up front and knelt at the communion rail. Mary not being a Catholic nonetheless opened and read from the Church Missal available in the pews.

A few minutes later, Mary got up and walked into the small adjacent room where there is a "hole" in the ground containing what is believed by some to be "holy soil." (Even though the Church itself does not credit it formally as such, many worshippers who have a deep faith adorn the walls with special prayers and keepsakes as testimonials to the healing soil.)

The walls of the room, roughly 15' by 45' in width and length, are covered with two or three layers of mementos from those who claimed to have been recipients of miracles at the Santuario. Many were asking for God's holy protection for others, reinforcing their prayer requests with hundreds of photos of military service members and law enforcement officers.

As I was finishing my prayers at the communion rail, I looked up at the entrance to the side room and saw Mary standing there motioning me to come into the room.

I finished my prayers and went into the room, bowing my head in order not to hit the top of the small entrance.

As I walked into the room, I abruptly stopped in front of Mary. Before she could say anything I felt my head being turned around and my gaze being directed to one "poster." It was a picture of Jesus with outstretched hands wearing a golden and white robe. The scripture from Isaiah 49:16 beamed out to us, "Fear not, for you are indelibly enscribed in the palms of My hands."

Mary then shared with me that when she walked into that room, her gaze had also been turned to that one poster. It was as though the poster was the only thing hanging on the wall when, in fact, there were hundreds of photos, letters, scapulars, beads, rosaries and other assorted items two-three deep along the 60-70 feet of walls as testimonials of people's faith.

At the time I was not familiar with the scripture, "Fear not, for you are indelibly enscribed in the palms of My hands." Mary, steeped in the knowledge of the scriptures, was quite familiar with Isaiah 49:16 and told me that just before she got up from the pew to go into the side room, she had prayed to God that He would hold us in His hands and show us what His will was concerning our relationship: should we work on building a relationship, or, should we "move on?"

Prayer answered? Miracle? For us, most definitely!

The specific words that we both saw on the poster, "indelibly enscribed," reinforced for us the fact that God had answered the prayer.

Interestingly, we have not found those specific words anywhere else. The word "enscribed" as we saw it on the poster is typically spelled with an "I" as "inscribed." Likewise, we have found that the most popular versions of this scripture have a different description, usually one of the following words: engraved, etched, written, carved, or graven. None have had the adverb "indelibly."

Nor have we found the image we saw, with Jesus' head and shoulders as the background and His two hands extended forward. Everything we have found has Jesus with only one hand extended. Occasionally, we have found pictures of two hands "floating," with no attachment to a body.

We have searched Christian book stores in all the cities we have visited, looking for anything with Jesus and His two hands extended forward and the specific words and spellings, "indelibly enscribed."

This miracle is coincident with what we consider to be our marriage day. Irrespective of any civil union, that is the day that God joined us as one.

When we went back to the Santuario a year later we did not find the "poster" in that side room. When we asked the volunteers who work there what they may have done with the poster, none of them had any memory of anything resembling our "poster," neither did the resident priest. It was as though God placed it there for just the two of us, reinforcement for us, God's wedding gift to us.

We recently celebrated our true twentieth wedding anniversary on September 18th. Civilly, our wedding anniversary is on January 2nd.

The Jacket

The last miracle I mention is one that can more easily be argued to be simply coincidental, but please hear me out.

Over a year ago, I lost my small key ring with seven small keys on the ring. At the time, I had been walking two to three miles a day on the sidewalk around our house. I often took the keys out of the desk drawer so that I could pick up the mail from the mail box across the street from our house.

On one particular day as I began to cross the street to get the mail, the key ring was nowhere to be found. I searched the desk drawers, the floor around the desk ... anywhere that I might have put the key ring down.

For the next 10 days, I scoured the area around the sidewalk which was covered with quarter inch gravel looking for anything shiny, hopefully attached to a key ring. I also looked in our back yard where I often alternated my walking path. In this case, half of my walking path consisted of good old dusty earth. I shuffled and kicked my feet thinking that perhaps I had dropped the key ring and it had been covered with soil or dust. Nothing!

I also dug in our compost bin in case the key ring had fallen out of my shirt pocket while I was aerating the bin. Again, nothing.

Two months later I stopped looking.

Today, more than a year later, I was in a hurry to run down to the post office before it closed since I needed to mail a birthday card to my granddaughter, SFC.

As I headed out to the garage to get the car, my wife asked me if I were going to put on a jacket since winter weather had recently arrived.

A bit exasperated that I had neglected to get my jacket, I rushed to the coat closet and reached for my favorite jacket, one that is appropriate for the days transitioning from autumn to winter.

As I put the jacket on, I hurriedly went to kiss my wife when I noticed her looking at me with a quizzical look.

"I thought you didn't like that jacket."

When she said that, I stopped and looked at the jacket. It did have a bit of a different feel from my favorite jacket. Also, the appalling appearance with the loud, shiny blue and white stripe on the sleeves going around the back of the jacket *and* around the chest of the jacket made me jerk with a sneer.

I just shrugged my shoulders, however, and said to Mary, "Okay, God is sending me a message that I need to wear this jacket." I had never worn this jacket in the 10 years since my father had given it to me. It had gone into the stack of curious gifts that Mom or Pop must have bought for me when they were on sale. You know, yellow and pink socks, a burgundy knit sweater that might have fit me as an eight-year old (I was in my 30s or 40s). But my Mom never let a good sale go to waste!

I had not included this jacket with the other clothes we had donated to a charity since it was one of many of my father's too-ugly-or-not-useful gifts which he gave with good intentions. Perhaps I would donate it to a charity on the tenth anniversary of his joining my mother in heaven?!

As I looked at the jacket with mild disdain, we both just sort of smiled, but I decided not to change since I was in a hurry and besides I was just going to the post office and was unlikely to see anyone who might see me wearing this hideous jacket.

As I resumed my steps out to the garage, I felt a small bulge in one of the pockets.

No way!

The bulge? It was the "lost" ring of keys with the mail box key!

If God weren't smiling that time!?!

Keys over a year lost! Found in a jacket which had **never** been worn! (The day I lost the keys was near the end of spring, clearly not jacket weather! I recall wearing my typical walking clothes, shorts and a T-shirt. There was absolutely no reason to have been wearing a jacket.)

If you feel there is a coincidence there, good for you! I'm going to stick with knowing that God likes to joke, like He did when Mack stepped off the dock and instantly sank into the water. (Ya gotta read *The Shack* to find out what that is about.)

I'm sure that if God laughs, He just had a small laugh. Maybe it was one of the angels assigned to occasionally travel with us who did it. Some of them *are* stinkers who love to not be serious around us.

So Many Miracles

Today I realize that in addition to the special miracles I just described, I am actually "swimming" in miracles: the way the earth spins on a precise axis, working with the sun to heat and cool the earth in mind-boggling ways; the way the sun, moon and stars share light with us is not only functional but so beautiful.

There are so many other miracles that God has sprinkled around us to enjoy. I imagine God watches us and smiles when we discover another of His miracles.

One of God's least appreciated miracles? How about that cover around our bodies? It tans, it stretches, *and* most importantly it keeps all of our innards from just spilling out. We call it "skin." How about that?

As mysteriously, how do those hydrogen molecules know that they need two of them to bond with one oxygen molecule in order to produce water!?! Another taken-for-granted miracle. And the way the blood vessels travel through our bodies delivering just the right product, e.g., oxygen to our brains so that we can process thoughts, wisdom, and facts?

There are so many miracles that we just take for granted, and for which I do not thank God often enough.

The biggest miracle of all, that God loves each and every one of us ... unconditionally! Now *that* is a miracle. Really, is any single one of us that loveable! Well, maybe my grandmother ... and new-born babies? But for the rest of us, God's unconditional love *is indeed* a miracle.

Point Of Reference

(Hand Towel)

One of the best lessons I ever learned happened on a lonely road in eastern Arizona.

My then friend (who became my wife a year later) and I were driving down a somewhat steep, gravelly hillside road when she suddenly began screaming at me to slow down.

I unfortunately screamed back, "What do you mean, slow down? I'm not speeding!"

After arguing about whether I were driving too fast, she suddenly more quietly stated, "I'm sorry but that's my point of reference."

At first I was fully confused, what do you mean, "That's your point of reference?"

Her reply was that she *felt* I was driving too fast. She was no longer screaming, but she was clearly upset.

Her serious and now-quiet tone of voice stopped me in my tracks and I thought to myself, "If I love this person and she *feels* that I am driving too fast, then for her, I *am* driving too fast. Whether I am or not driving too fast is not the point; that is irrelevant. If I love her and she is scared for whatever reason, then I need to respond as though what she *feels* must also become my point of reference."

I pulled her little white Toyota pick-up off the road, stopped the engine, and turned to her.

Although we were fully grown, confident adults, all I saw was a frightened woman. For some unknown reason, seeing the look on her face moved me to take her hand and gently ask her why she felt that I was going too fast.

As it turned out, she had been frightened as a young child by someone who was driving their vehicle too fast. She could not recall any details other than it scared her.

As I waited for her to offer more explanation, I saw that same frightened little girl sitting in the passenger's seat. She was no longer the 5' 8" confident and attractive young lady seated next to me; now she was just a frightened little girl.

After a few minutes, she said she didn't want to talk about it any longer.

She asked me to promise to slow down. With a concerned tear in my eye, I promised her that I would never drive too fast again.

I explained, however, that there might be times when she would have to tell me that she felt I was driving too fast, and I asked her to promise me that she would say something *before* she felt she had to scream at me.

For the next 20-plus years, we have both kept our promises.

In the ensuing years, it has been helpful for her *and* for me to understand that what one of us "knows to be the truth," may not be the truth for the other. (I suppose this is along the lines of that parable about two or more blind men touching an elephant and describing what "it was" in totally different ways.) While I first heard that story a long time ago, I never had thought of it as becoming a part of my experience. In fact I must admit that in my teens and twenties, I *knew* what was true, and no one else better challenge my knowledge. Wow, there's that ego again!

It has helped both of us to use that "point of reference" explanation when confronting an incident of disagreement. I must admit that there have been times when I felt she was missing the point so I have offered that same mantra, "I'm sorry but that is my point of reference." ☺

It is important enough that we make sure that we do not abuse that. It is simply a method of fully respecting the other person's feelings irrespective of the *actual* reality.

Reflections - Using Basic Skills

(Hand Towel)

Some background about *unused towels*: Just as there are under-valued towels, e.g., wash cloths, so are there under-valued skills and talents which most of us have, but we don't think of them as having much value. Wash cloths are seldom the kind of "towels" to which much value is given. "I could have used my hand." Of what real value are they?

The same goes for some under-valued skills and talents that the Good Lord has loaned us. A gentle smile, a nod of acknowledgement, listening; of what value are they? It is interesting that when these things are shared, they stand out ... not so much because of the smile or gentle nod, but because the other person is *being acknowledged.*

The three examples which I share below stand out as prime examples where simple, basic skills produced wonderful results. No special skills were used. They include situations dealing with a diverse assortment of persons: (1) "unruly" teenagers, (2) battered women, and (3) successful professionals.

The frameworks for these three cases were generated by: (1) my being able to connect with bored teenagers who were scheduled to spend time with this old guy (me), probably to give the Boys and Girls Club staff an hour break; (2) my being able to make several women feel good about themselves after they had been convinced they were worthless, and so they ended up in a battered women's shelter; and (3) my being able to assist an office full of attorneys who made their living communicating with and persuading their clients to achieve a common point of view, yet were unable to do so for themselves, to the point that they were on the brink of going out of business.

The successful, ensuing results were not due to my use of superior talents and skills, but due to simple, basic connections with the folks involved: listening, giving respect in a friendly, non-judgmental way, and listening (*listening* is so important; this has to be emphasized).

Reflecting On Helping Kids From Several Boys & Girls Clubs

At one time in my life I was not financially able to donate money to community organizations as I had been able to do in previous years. The thought that I might have something more valuable than money to donate made me think that some of my skills could be of value to others. The Boys and Girls Clubs in town came to mind. I set up an appointment with one of their staff to see what I might be able to offer. When we met I mentioned that I wanted to volunteer my time in some way that might help the kids. I mentioned that one of the skills I had developed was public speaking and I asked if the kids, mostly from low-income or ethnic minority communities, could benefit from gaining greater self-confidence through being able to better communicate with others.

My reason for focusing on building their self-confidence was based on my own inadequacies as a teenager and eventually as a young adult.

At the age of 30 I was still too shy to look someone in the eyes when talking with them. If I were talking with a man, I would typically look at his chest. If it were a woman, I would look at her forehead.

So at this "mature" age of 30, I joined a local Toastmasters club. After several harrowing weeks of standing in front of the group, "speaking" about the "Table Topics For The Day" (with the "Uh!" buzzer sounding for the entire sixty seconds that I was required to stand), I almost quit. However, I had recently been promoted to a position that required me to meet with lots of strangers in various cities throughout the state, including politicians and the news media, and so I persevered.

God helped me survive the first weeks of the weekly Toastmaster meetings and pretty soon, my confidence level soared. I began winning the weekly "Best Speaker" and "Most Improved Speaker" awards at my chapter. (I say "weekly" even though we were typically scheduled only once every six weeks or so. My confidence level was such that when a scheduled speaker did not show up, I would volunteer to take his place, having already prepared several speeches in advance from the TI manual.) There was even one week where I replaced two of the three scheduled speakers winning "Best Speaker" with one speech and "Most Improved Speaker" with the other speech. I had found "my niche," albeit at the advanced age of 30.

I wondered what my life might have been if I'd had *any* self-confidence in my earlier years. I wanted to do what I could for kids at the Boys and Girls Clubs who many, like me, had no true role models from whom to learn self-confidence in speaking in front of others.

It seemed that I was there at a good time since they were getting ready to have their City Youth of the Year competition. One of the major requirements was that the contestants give a short speech to a panel of volunteer judges, typically business people, teachers or politicians. This was a month or two before the various clubs would be competing to select their Club Youth of the Year. The various club winners would then compete on a city-wide basis to select the City Youth of the Year who would later compete for the State Youth of the Year.

Interestingly, when I approached the staff overseeing the four clubs in town, they looked at one another with a measure of curiosity. I indicated that I would like a 60-to-90-minute time period for these "classes" with the kids. They all laughed and one of the male staff somewhat derisively replied that I would be lucky to keep their attention for 30 minutes. I noticed that all the staff were "born of privilege" where they likely had plenty of role models for most aspects of their lives. I unambiguously told them that I would not do this unless I had at least a sixty-minute time period with the kids.

When they saw how firm and serious I was, they basically acquiesced *saying* "Okay, go ahead." I learned later they were thinking to themselves, "Yeah, okay go ahead. Then after a week or two after trying to keep a room full of 14 to 17 year-old boys and girls interested, when they could be back at their respective clubs playing ping-pong or basketball, or, 'just hanging out,' you'll see what we're talking about and then we can go back to the half-hour schedule."

As it turned out, the 60 minutes was insufficient. When the word got around, all the clubs began requesting to be included whenever possible, always wanting to stay longer than the scheduled time. However, the club transport vans were having to wait to take them back to their own clubs; and so, we were forced to limit the sessions to two hours, moving the meeting locations from one club to another club on succeeding weeks. (During the five years I was able to help, only one "tough" young man walked out of any of the sessions. The rest were a bundle of unbridled pleasure to meet with. Tall, short, serious, laughing, smiling, each with his or her individual, unique beauty! All "future contributors" to what makes this country great! All "destined for greatness!")

I set about helping the kids under the auspices that I was there to help the kids who would be competing for Club Youth of the Year. I emphasized to the kids in the first sessions, however, that while there would only be one winner from each club, that *all of them* were speakers on a daily basis in their everyday lives. Therefore a greater self-confidence would benefit each of them, i.e., making presentations in their classes, talking with their parents, or with their bosses, or with other kids (e.g., that cute guy or gal they would like to meet).

I typically got their attention with my personal story of lacking any self-confidence well past my teenage years. That I could not look anyone in the eyes puzzled them. When I explained about looking at men's chests but women's foreheads, the ice would be broken as they chuckled and punched one another in the arm.

Delightfully, the kids always had to be told that their vans were waiting to take them back to their clubs, and so they reluctantly had to leave. I will always remember the fist-bumps, hugs, nods, or "thank you" as they left.

Part of the reason why the sessions were so popular and successful was that I shared with them basic skills. They "saw" that I was not a big, powerful, dynamic speaker; I *was* an adult version of them.

Although I had not endured the same social environment which many of them had experienced growing up, I clearly "felt" what they had endured growing up. Indirectly, I sensed their basic emotions. Many things in these teenagers' lives had taught them to be suspicious and fear others, their facial and body expressions hardened against the chance of an encounter with anyone who might not welcome them openly.

I started each new class with the basics of public speaking, customizing the Toastmasters training which I had received by slowly working up to their circumstances, focused on enhancing their self-esteem. I would begin with simple lessons, e.g., at first there were no time constraints and they did not have to "stand up" to answer questions like "What is your favorite color?" or "What is your favorite food?"

Key to all the lessons, however, was an emphasis on challenging them to think as individuals and not as part of any peer group. Reinforcing self-confidence was fundamental to being able to think as individuals; importantly, this reinforcement had to be relevant to their current circumstances balanced with where they might want to be when "fully accomplished, not necessarily 'perfect,' but with an expanding goal of achieving the highest ambitions they could attain."

Gradually I would have them stand to talk and I also gave them a topic and a time frame, e.g., "What is your favorite animal and why? You must stand for 60 seconds. If you do not wish to talk, you still have to stand until I tell you the 60 seconds is up."

After a while, the topics became more detailed, but always related to their circumstances. "Tell us what makes you happy, e.g., riding a horse, going shopping at the mall, going to your chemistry class, working on your car." Also, they now had to speak for three minutes while standing in front of the group.

During one of these sessions, I asked the question, "What makes you most happy?" One young man shared how he hated to say it but what made him most happy was when his father got drunk ... "because that is the only time he talks to me with some affection, instead of as a disciplinarian or a judge of my failures."

Another time I will always remember was when the kids were asked to talk for 3-5 minutes about the most important person in their life.

The following heartbreaking response happened after I had called on all the kids in the room except for one young man. "Michael" was one of the few non-ethnic minority kids, a tall strawberry blond, 16-17 years old, dressed in new, well-ironed clothes.

His response was, "My mother is the most important person in my life. She works so hard and she doesn't get any breaks." Holding back tears, he went on with more details about how she sacrificed to raise him as a single mother. "She gets up early in the morning, fixes me breakfast and lunch, then goes back to bed for an hour before going out to her second job. At the end of the day, she is always waiting for me. I sometimes have to wake her up so that we can eat dinner. On weekends, she does the laundry and cleans house. The only time she goes out of the house is to do the grocery shopping." He went on with more personal things he appreciated from her, e.g., not buying new clothes for herself so that she could buy him new clothes.

"I wish I had more time to spend with her, doing things together. I wish I could buy her gifts, like a new blouse, really anything that would make her smile, flowers, candy, a card."

When he finished, he had everyone in the room (14–17-year-olds) and me in tears.

We all sat there silently until I heard the shuffle of one person getting up from her chair. She walked over and hugged him quietly until some of the other kids joined her. She was also a tall young lady, about 16 years old. (Importantly at the time I recall that this pretty young lady was one who I remember as basically stoic, virtually emotionless in previous sessions. I also remember how her beautiful dark brown skin contrasted with his almost pale reddish skin. She was one of God's wonderful creations with a God-Given Tan, someone with what I refer to as GGT*.)

While the kids were sharing "Michael's" grief, my heart was full of guilt because I had not called on the young man since I erroneously assumed that he would have no "big" issues like all the other ethnically minority kids in the group.

This assumption that he would not have the degree of "deep issues" like the other kids was based on various private conversations that many of the kids sought me out to talk about. Sadly, too many of them had experienced having friends or relatives die in their arms, sometimes from gang violence, sometimes from drive-by shootings. One kid talked with me because he had been contemplating suicide because he thought he might be gay because of a same-gender sexual encounter.

As it turned out, "Michael" expressed the same un-spoken appreciation that all the other kids had for their parents, many of them single mothers or fathers. This young man was inwardly just like them. His deep emotions spoke for all of the kids!

* I prefer "GGT" for "God-Given Tan" instead of "Black" or "African-American." (Some of the most beautiful women I have met were indeed black. Most, however, have been *varying lighter shades* of stunning black, or varying shades of gorgeous brown. Nor do I know whether they are direct descendants from Africa, or possibly sharing other ethnic backgrounds.) Most of us strive to get some darker pigmentation in our skin; we call it "sun tanning." This young lady by the grace of God was given her darker skin when she was born; she did not have to go through the extra effort to get "that nice tan" like many of us do.

I will always remember each of them. I will especially remember one of them, the pretty, bubbly young lady, Vila, 17 years old, her eyes radiating gregarious, contagious optimism of "more good things to happen," far removed from the dangerous escape when she was six years old, through dark rivers and hazardous lands to escape from Laos, and then from one refugee camp to another until arriving in the United States.

Unlike her, the majority of "the kids" were born and raised in the vicinity of their clubs, but who, for years, did not feel that they would be welcomed at the Club; nonetheless, wishing and wondering what it would be like to go there. Finally one of the kind, big-hearted Boys and Girls Club staff members would persuade them to "join us."

Again, no special skills were needed to help these young ladies and gentlemen. The "basic under-valued skills" I used were listening, giving respect in a friendly, non-judgmental way, talking with them about things that were *important to them* **and** to their futures without "preaching," validating them as individuals, and yes, **listening** to their thoughts and concerns.

Note: Sweet Vila would go on to win City Youth of the Year, and a few months later, State Youth of the Year.

Note: More about "black" and GGT (God-Given Tan). This seems to be a good place to share a special story.

One of the most naturally loving persons I have ever met was Mrs. Jones, a soul who I met when I moved to Kansas for a job. How we met and why is not relevant to "our involvement."

What is relevant is that although I was new to her town, we bonded quickly and she soon began calling me her "Number One Son" even though she had her own biological son.

She *was* one woman I knew who could definitely be described as "black." She was the quintessential living model of "Black Is Beautiful!"

She often invited me and my girlfriend over for her spirited Sunday dinners full of genuine camaraderie and wonderful laughter, where people from her church as well as friends and neighbors drifted in and out of her house over the afternoon. [My girlfriend and I were the only persons in the house who needed to lie in the sun to get a tan. Everyone else was blessed with that GGT (God-Given Tan).]

Although I moved back to Arizona about a year later, our friendship had become a caring one. A year after moving back to Arizona, she and a female friend came to visit me for two weeks. When I asked her what she would like to do while she was visiting me, she gave me a long wish list that included visits to the Grand Canyon, Las Vegas and Disneyland. The only one we could not include was the long trek to Disneyland.

While staying with me in Phoenix, she and I joined my parents who had come to travel with us to visit the Grand Canyon and Las Vegas. Before my parents returned home, I took the three of them to dinner at Pinnacle Peak, north of Scottsdale. This western steak house was known for cutting off the ties of "gentlemen" and pinning the "cut ties" to the ceiling and wall.

They also were known for their disdain for anyone ordering their steak "well done."

Knowing that my mother and Mrs. Jones both would order their steaks "well done," I had my camera ready to snap a picture of the two of them as the servers simultaneously lifted the serving dome food covers off all our plates. When the plate covers came off their dinner plates, Mrs. Jones and my mother were each staring at a really ugly, old beat-up cowboy boot laying right in front of them.

My mother shrieked as though she had been served a dead mouse. Mrs. Jones stayed quiet but her eyes seemed to grow larger, highlighting the large radiant whites in her eyes against the very black iris in her eyes. The contrast of her beautiful black skin and my mother's equally beautiful, but almost pale-white skin was divinely exceptional. This is a photograph which I highly treasure, one to be highly cherished for a lifetime, a photograph of two special women of whom I was "especially fond" (to quote Poppa in *The Shack*).

Reflecting On Encouraging Women
At A Battered Women's Shelter
To See Themselves In A Positive Way

This was one of my saddest experiences in helping others in my life.

I had called the local battered women's shelter to see if there were some way that I could help their clients. Having been vetted by the local Boys and Girls Club and having had a successful experience with the kids in helping them increase their levels of confidence, I thought I might be able to help the women who were required to find a job and a place to live within three months of arriving at the women's shelter.

I began by holding group sessions geared to helping them gain or increase their self-confidence in basic communication skills. I used the same basic skills that I had used with the kids at the Boys and Girls

Clubs: *listening*, giving respect in a friendly, non-judgmental way. However, it was not the same environment as that at the Boys and Girls Clubs.

I will never forget the looks on their faces, suspicious of a male who was there to *help* them. "What's in it for you? Why should we believe that you want to help us?"

Since I was still in the throes of a new mental state of "knowing that *I* will never trust another woman again," I could strangely empathize with them and with their suspicions.

Their faces clearly reflected how beat down they felt, but I was not there to change their entire lives. I emphasized that I only hoped to help them get a kick-start in finding a job that paid more than entry level positions at fast food eating places. Since they were all facing a 90-day deadline for finding a job and somewhere to live, they reluctantly accepted my assistance.

I quickly found that most of them had no confidence in being interviewed for a job, especially if it were a male doing the interview, or even a *demanding* female. Since most of the jobs these women felt qualified for were hourly-wage jobs, the majority of the job interviews they had were conducted by people who were not particularly sensitive to these women. Their lack of self-confidence was often heightened by a life-time of having been abused by husbands or boyfriends who typically bullied the women.

It became evident that helping them was not going to be easy since just about every one of them could not *see* themselves as worthwhile. It therefore became important to find a way that I could get them to *see themselves on paper.* In addition, only one of the women I helped had a resume. She was a very attractive, confident young lady with a Master's degree, yet here she was. None of the rest of the women had a resume to present when going for an interview.

When I asked the group whether they would prefer to continue the group practice interviews we had been doing, or, whether they would prefer individual (one on one) rehearsal interviews for a specific job, they all chose the individual rehearsal interviews.

What followed was the Shelter calling me when any of the women had a job interview coming up for which they wanted to schedule a rehearsal interview with me.

The first thing I did was to go through the steps to develop a resume they could take with them. I asked simple questions about their skills and unfortunately I often ran into blank stares when I asked about their skill strengths. Eventually I got them to tell me things they did in their daily lives. I then translated those daily experiences into skill strengths, e.g., managing a family budget with less income than expenses became "budgeting experience."

Eventually, I was able to produce for each one at least a one-page summary of bullets identifying their strong points.

Invariably when I printed out their resumes and they saw what I had summarized as their skills and strengths, they would say, "but that is not me." I would then repeat the answers they had given me earlier and little by little, they became a bit more convinced that the resume skills did in fact reflect them.

At a minimum, the written resumes gave them indirect *support* about positive aspects of themselves. I encouraged them to look at the resumes as much as they could before the interviews so they might eventually *see* themselves as the person described in their resume.

Again, there were no special skills used to help them; the basic skills were simply *listening*, and giving respect in a friendly, non-judgmental way. Regretfully, the objective was only to help them get a job. Hopefully, this little step in seeing themselves differently created a more positive self-image and an improved self-confidence.

Reflecting On Helping An Office Full Of Attorneys Trained To Persuade Others To Achieve A Common Point Of View But Who Were Unable To Do It For Themselves

The basic skills used: *listening*, giving respect in a friendly, non-judgmental way.

Another example of using only basic skills involved a Founding Partner at a major law firm which had asked me to help them as they were struggling with a variety of issues so dire that they were forced to cancel their annual, very popular Christmas party for clients and staff. The cancellation was mainly due to their concern about their decreasing income revenue stream which contributed to a rising strife within the partnership.

I had been approached by one of the partners of the law firm who had participated in a pro-bono weekend retreat that I had conducted for the local Girl Scouts Board. After the retreat, he asked me if I did "that kind of workshop" for businesses. I laughed and replied, "Yes, I have to make money somewhere; this weekend retreat was free."

He said he would like me to meet the partners at his law firm who were looking for some way to resolve their internal conflicts. At the time, this was the largest law firm in a town of 500,000.

My typical approach to situations like this was to assess what the actual issues really were, and how serious they were. I had found out that most of the time when I was called on to help with a certain "problem," the real problem was very different from what they described as the issue with which they wanted my help. I typically had to identify the real problem so that I was not merely treating the symptom of the problem but that I was addressing the full problem. (It is not that difficult to *treat* the symptom of the problem. That is one way to assure job security for the problem solver; "See you again in a few months!")

In this case, I scheduled one-to-two hour interviews with each of the partners, the associates, the office manager, and a few other key staff, e.g., certain clerks and personal secretaries. I also added to the initial list anyone whose name surfaced more than once during the initial interviews.

The interviews were all efficient and successful enough that the partners hurriedly scheduled a two-day weekend retreat at one of the partner's homes.

Unfortunately, there was one person who refused to meet with me, the one remaining active Founding Partner. (One Founding Partner had recently passed away and the other had retired years earlier.) Being the only remaining Founding Partner, he carried more authority than the other partners.

His refusal to meet with me forced me to tell his partners that I would not conduct the weekend retreat until I had met with him.

His partners, each having spent two to three hours with me in preparation for their weekend retreat, pressured him to meet with me.

At the appointed time, he grudgingly let me into his office and then immediately began to grill me about my law experience and whether I had ever done this with any other law firms. In about ten minutes, his secretary came in, and obviously "pre-planned," told him that he had an important phone call.

He surprised her by telling her to tell the caller he would call him back. In another hour, the secretary came back in and told him that his next appointment was waiting for him. He again surprised her when he told her to reschedule that person *and* to cancel the rest of his appointments that afternoon.

When we walked out of his office after about four hours, his partners were standing nearby to see what had happened. He just looked at all of them, and exclaimed, "This is the best therapy I've ever experienced!"

This is another example where no special skills were used. *Listening* with respect helped to get the partners committed to a mutual goal.

The following year they were back to hosting the most festive holiday celebration in the city during the holidays.

So This Is What It's Like Getting Old

(Beach Towel)

The Basics

I get to wear unmatched PJs, and nobody cares or notices.

I get to wear white socks with sandals and (I hope) nobody notices or cares.

Also as I told my Dad when he was in his 80s, " 'the gals' are not hugging you because you are that young stud off the farm who enthralled my mother when she first saw you sixty years ago. Now they hug you because you're 'a cute old man.'"

An Older Person's Lament/Request

One older person's lament/request: "I want you to stop asking me, 'Are you okay?' when I'm just sitting, resting, or, stopping to look around."

I cannot believe how many times this has happened in my life as I have gotten more gray/white haired. As a matter of fact, it just happened again a few minutes ago as I was waiting for my wife to exit the ladies room.

(This was at the Hilton Waikoloa, which abounds with gorgeous, colorful birds that one seldom sees back on "the mainland.")

As I waited, I noticed a beautiful, fuzzy-red-topped, little bird with a pure white breast and black wings as it unhurriedly hunted and pecked for little goodies off the sidewalk. I decided to share the experience by leaning against a column and watching my new, little BF.

Suddenly, a hotel worker stopped, tapped me on the shoulder and quietly asked, "Are you okay? Do you need help?" I politely replied that I was okay. She looked down, smiled and walked away. I thought, "Thank you, Mam, but if I were not white-haired, would you have assumed something was wrong?"

Months later, in the parking lot of my neighborhood Albertsons, I was looking into the trunk of my car pondering how many cloth bags to take inside so as to not use the plastic bags that the store provides.

Suddenly, I looked to my right as a woman was *running* towards me, *hollering*, "Are you okay? Are you okay?"

While I appreciated her concern, she scared me such that I looked around to see who needed help. (If I am clearly in distress, go ahead and make a fuss, but please make sure it is clear that I am in distress before calling out the army. *Mama mia! Dios mio! Oi vey!*)

When I told my 91-½ year old mother-in-law (She is very proud of having made it to the half-year; I thought only pre-teens did that.) about those two incidents, she said, "I'd appreciate the fact that someone was nice enough to check on me."

Hmmmm. You're right, Mom, I'm sure there will come a day when I will share that sentiment. But in the meantime, please make sure that "the old person" you're rushing up "to save" is truly in distress and not just "being old."

My Collection Of "Tuits" Continues To Grow

Since I now have lots of free time as I am now retired, with no meetings to prepare for, phone calls to make or return, no business trips to prepare for or undertake, I realize that I have lots of time to get things taken care of.

This has unfortunately resulted in my collection of "Tuits" growing quickly. (You know, I'll get around "to it" when I actually care to get it done. ☺)

I Wonder

As Mary and I were doing a final edit of this manuscript, I became more aware of how "almost tipping over" cups was so infuriating for me. I began to wonder whether the tendency to "almost tip" over cups was a sign of getting old. Having early macular degeneration, I wonder whether ageing has affected my depth perception; that might indicate that I am not reaching far enough. I suppose this could be a silent frustration of getting old. Hmmm, I'll have to ask my doctor about that. (BTW, a wonderful phrase popped up as I was researching this; instead of using the word "elderly," the phrase "later adulthood" was used. Even though they use "later adulthood" as beginning at the age of 40, I think I may borrow it as a substitute where I use the word "elderly.")

Starters, Doers and Finishers

(Hand Towel)

One important lesson I learned when I was in put charge of a project team or office was to focus on whether we had a good balance of "Starters, Doers and Finishers."

Sometimes I was short of Starters; we could never seem to "get going."

Other times I had too many Doers but no Finishers; the projects were late and over budget.

This lesson was especially helpful when I was brought in to do some trouble shooting, a few times being charged with more than simply identifying the solution to "the stated problem," but further given the responsibility to carry out "cleaning up" an unacceptable situation.

Normally, I was called into an office or project team with an already established staff. About half the time, the office or company I was asked to help was dealing with product delivery and/or income issues. Sometimes it was just a team needing a project manager. Many times I assisted as outside help, aka "consultant."

As such it was standard that I had to figure out why I had been asked to help out; the supposed reasons for bringing me in were often not reflective of what was actually going on. More often it was due to some sort of unapparent mismanagement; classically "headquarters" became concerned only when they began losing money and therefore "the problem" had developed slowly over time.

I learned early on that my first objective needed to be to find out "What is actually going on."

Surprisingly, it did not usually take too much effort to ferret out the facts. More often than not, the key people to aid in resolving the "problem" were the support staff and frequently the office manager, but they were seldom asked for their input, and when asked, their input was regularly disregarded by "the professionals." Sadly, they had learned to give the answers that the "powers-that-be" were looking for, or, to temper their responses with information that was neither complete nor "too negative."

This made my job easier; respect *all* the folks on the staff and find out from them what was *actually* going on. Their honest input to me made my "research and assessment" quite efficient. "Gee, Fil, how were you able to find out what was really going on? No one told us what you just told us." (I quietly wondered, "Did you bother to respect 'the little people' enough to truly listen to them, or, did you just walk away after you heard what you wanted to hear?")

When tasked with the responsibility of overseeing the "clean-up on aisle five," I had to delve deeper than simply identifying the full issues/problems and to take it to the next step, implementing an acceptable solution.

This is when I also learned to discreetly assess whether there was a correct balance of Starters, Doers and Finishers to carry out the recommended solutions. It was critical that the "apparent issue" not only be resolved, but that the underlying situation which created the unacceptable situation in the first place be corrected.

Obviously, the staff's skills and talents were fundamental to doing the work; that was not usually the issue needing attention; most situations had perfectly talented staff. *The problem* characteristically was that they were running over budget, or, past time for completing the tasks. Since talent was not the issue, I had to intuitively figure out why they were in trouble.

Part of my learning curve was due to my own flaws. I love starting projects but I become distracted, "I have something else to start, I don't have time to finish this."

However, once started, I typically stayed on course with little wasted action. (That has been without a doubt the most often repeated feedback I have received since I turned my God-loaned talents to conducting workshops/classes: "I very much appreciated how you kept the discussions on course and the side conversations to a minimum." "I appreciated the efficiency with which you guided us to proper conclusions." "Thanks for taking over the discussions; we were all over the place until you took over.")

Thus, this vital mantra: assure a balance of Starters, Doers and Finishers in your talent pool.

One example: One of the first offices I was asked to "rescue" was an office in Orange County which had been very successful since its opening a few years earlier. As time went by, the original office manager (Title: Company President) began to "believe his press releases," and due to his early success soon became RIP, "Retired In Place."

His being attractive to potential and eventual clientele had earlier been judged by the parent company as an asset. However, it became a liability as he began spending most of his time "schlepping" potential clients without getting signatures or producing deliverables.

Apparently he was too busy entertaining that he never noticed that the contracts were going over-budget and/or were resulting in delayed deliveries. But, hey, a sumptuous dinner at an elegant restaurant in San Francisco, flown up in the company plane would take care of that.

Except that soon the clients began asking the worker-bees for contracted products and were getting none.

The ability of the original office manager to start but not finish projects eventually trickled over to his staff, who without any proper guidance, continued to research options and develop additional scenarios for the contracts on which they were working. They were seldom being asked for final products until it was too late. Expensive!

It was much more fun to think and dream than to actually finish especially when finishing a hum-drum project. The excitement was in the search and discovery. But once that was over with, getting down to work was much less fun. Besides one is seldom judged too harshly when "working on it," but once the work is done, here come the judgments, "not exactly what I was looking for."

In this particular office, I unfortunately had to "clean house." All except one young recent college graduate were replaced. She provided the carry-over stability having been a curious and fast learner. The staff was more than happy to "train" someone who appeared to be quite anxious to find out what they had been doing, and often to do the tedious "final" work. In this way she learned a lot about the work that the office was doing. A nice surprise and a very necessary asset.

One thing, however, that I did not recognize as I was hiring the replacement staff was that while I had achieved a balance of Starters, Doers and Finishers among the professional staff, I had not done that with the support staff. I soon found that the support staff were (literally) all Geminis like me. While there are certainly a wide variety of Geminis, this staff consisted of typical Geminis like me, predictably working on many things at once. While very productive, not the most efficient way to get specific work finished.

I therefore purposely set about to hire either a Virgo or a Capricorn as the office manager. (I know many folks do not put much stock in these astrological explanations; my wife is one. And for the most part I agree since I have often found that my "starting" is a typical Gemini trait, my "doing" and "finishing" are typical Virgo traits. When that inconsistency occurred in my life and I questioned a die-hard astrological devotee, "How can I be a Gemini – working on several tasks at one time but also being able to focus and get something done," the answer I got was that I "was probably born on the cusp." I'm not sure what being "born on the cusp" means, but "Hey, I had an explanation *and* I needed to finish." ☺)

(I must admit that one reason I enjoy this astrological moniker of being a Gemini is that I like not having to be a "one character" persona. It is fun to be my own twin! I josh! So, please don't get carried away with this. If you are troubled by this characterization, fret not! I do not check my astrological charts! Ever! But if ever you need organization, I strongly recommend finding yourself a Virgo, or, a Capricorn to manage organizing and producing the final product.)

Another project team which I inherited was a major, multi-dimensional, professional group consisting of engineers, planners, economic planners, and environmental planners. These folks came from seven major firms with personnel from 11 offices, many from out-of-state offices.

This project went extremely well although I had to eventually reduce the hours contracted to one firm whose Principals were in apparently high demand around the country. I found that contractually I could not terminate their contract, but I found that I could limit their hours to the point where they removed themselves from the contract.

This was a situation where the Principals were happy to "start" the work, thus allowing themselves to be billable, but who then skipped out on actual deliverables. Great Starters, certainly not Doers, and I never found out whether they were Finishers.

In the end, this project turned out to be one of the two highlights of my project management career. This was the result of a great team with the perfect balance of Starters, Doers and Finishers.

The other highlight of my project/office management career was one where I was allowed to hire the entire staff in order to start a new department. We accomplished a lot in a short time. We had one of the best balances of Starters, Doers and Finishers with whom I ever worked!

Unfortunately, I went from that highlight to the worst experience in my professional life, a situation where I inherited 75% of the staff, but found that the available hiring pool for the other 25% as well as for replacements was highly devoid of satisfactory talent, lacking in all three categories. It was difficult "starting," "doing," or "finishing" anything. We did it somehow and although the powers that be were happy with our work and after a year asked me to take the top spot in their organization, I recognized that I had already lowered my hiring standards in the year I had been there and I was not willing to continue to do that.

I left after 15 months. Not all situations are salvageable in an acceptable period of time.

A few additional thoughts about Starters, Doers and Finishers:

1) Very few persons are all three: Starters, Doers *and* Finishers.

2) Some of us are two of the three. We can *start* and *do*, but "chees," *finishing* takes a toll! Or, we can't get started but when the powers that be get the project started for us, or we inherit a project which is already started, watch out ... we are holy terrors – do not stand in the way! Or, we can *do* and *finish*, but *starting* is usually a debacle!

3) Unfortunately, many of us are only one of the three. We either enjoy starting, doing, or finishing; just don't ask us to do one of the others. We'll find a way to get bogged down one way or another.

4) My wife being a self-proclaimed "recovering perfectionist" opined that those who are able to start and do, but not finish, are likely perfectionists. After some discussion we agreed that a

perfectionist will continue improving the results to the point that finishing is almost impossible. Bottom line, most perfectionists are Starters and Doers but have a really tough time finishing. They may be forced to deliver something but are never truly *finished.*

5) In a business, not being able to finish is absolutely devastating. Contracts over budget! Deliverables late, or, incomplete! Poster businesses for "if you don't take care of this soon, you won't have to worry about it soon, cause you 'ain't gonna be in business' *soon*!"

6) The bottom line: In whatever project you are involved, assure that you have a proper balance of Starters, Doers and Finishers.

Suicide

(Bath Towel)

Please be advised that this is a very *heavy* discussion (*See Note Below). If reading this chapter at any time gets too heavy, I encourage you to take time out to *graze* with one of the lighter chapters, such as, "Embarrassing Moments," "Brief Encounters," or, "Thoughts, Personal." There are many funny and uplifting stories in those chapters to balance the gravity of this chapter. Grazing in one of those lighter chapters is something I have had to do several times as I am writing this. Many times, I read just one of the numerous short stories contained in those chapters. It *is* important to keep an optimistic heart.

Note: As I write this chapter, I am very aware that I am sometimes rambling, but rambling is the typical state of mind of one who is thinking about suicide. Straight-forward, rational thought is typically absent from someone seriously considering suicide. I also sometimes write as we all talk ... in incomplete sentences.

Also, I extend a sincere request, **if appropriate at any time** as you read this chapter or the chapter, "TOSTI," please stop reading and call the Suicide Prevention Line, currently 800.273.8255 (if a veteran, press 1). As of 16JUL22, one will also be able to dial 988 as a new 3-digit number to reach the National Suicide Prevention and Mental Crisis Lifeline.

Thoughts About Suicide

I have asked myself about each chapter in this book, "What is my objective in writing this chapter?"

I find the answer very easy in this case regarding suicide.

> Every time I hear of a combat veteran taking his or her life, I hurt.

> Every time I hear of a teenager being bullied to the point of taking her or his life, I hurt.

> Every time I hear of a lonely person overdosing, I hurt.

> Every time I hear of an elderly person being found dead with no one nearby with whom to talk, I hurt.

> Every time I hear about someone grievously suffering from low self-esteem, I hurt.

Every time I hear of a military spouse feeling overwhelmed, I hurt.

Every time I hear a family member or friend ask, "Where was the clue? ... How could I have missed the clue? ... I should have picked up on it ... if only she/he had given me a clue," not only do I hurt, **I ALSO WANT TO SCREAM!**

Having been to the depths of *pre-suicide* three times, plus having been prepared three times to *transition*, not just thinking about it but razor blade in hand and the determined reminder, "be sure to cut deep enough," I hurt.

Because of my own experiences, I know fully well that it is difficult to find someone with whom to share this hurt.

Some sobering and very disturbing statistics: in 2019, the Substance Abuse and Mental Health Services Administration (SAMHSA) reported that:

12 million adults had serious thoughts about suicide

3.5 million adults made plans to commit suicide

1.4 million adults attempted suicide

217,000 adults made no plans and attempted suicide

In 1997, 75% of elderly suicides visited their primary care doctors in the month before they committed suicide.

Note added on *May 27, 2021*: It was reported that 17 veterans take their lives *every day*.

I also know that when a well-meaning person makes the conditions worse by saying or doing the wrong thing, their actions or words toss the already despondent person even deeper into despair. Unfortunately, when one passes a certain point (*preparing* for one's final act – not just *thinking* about it), any little disturbance/depression can send one into that final spiral; "What you just did proves that this is the only action I can control."

Ask anyone who has been prepared, or, has gone through to their "final act" and survived it, they would likely tell you that the hurt never really goes away for good. They would tell you that *if* they felt comfortable talking with you about it, they would.

Based on my own experiences, I did just the opposite; I told no one how deeply sad I was. Instead, I pretended to be in good spirits and that "everything was just peachy." I did not want friends to remember me as a sad person. I wanted their final memories of me to be "He was such a fun guy!"

And so my objective in writing this chapter is to offer a brief incursion into one person's voyage into "the other side." I do not pretend to offer sage advice which would cure anyone or dissuade anyone from transitioning, but I do hope to make a difference, even a minor difference in at least one person's life ("a minor difference" is sometimes what it takes).

I am also fully aware that much has been written by and about people who have considered suicide, successfully or not. The accounts by those intimately involved in our mutual brother/sisterhood are much more moving than those written by so-called professionals.

One common factor in all of our stories is that while all these myriad of accounts are out there, many still continue to contemplate, prepare for, or, take the final step. And so I sadly join those writing or speaking in the hopes of reaching at least one person with words of encouragement that their life is worth staying alive for, and hopefully convincing that person that there is still work for that person to do on this earth. Nonetheless, I do not condemn anyone who does take that final step; instead I continue to pray for them.

Perhaps my thoughts will be of some encouragement for at least one person to stay afloat long enough to figure out how to escape from their depths. Possibly the encouragement will come through prayer, or, perhaps through an angel-messenger sent to help one realize that "You matter ... a lot!" If even one person chooses to live rather than transition, and not hurt, I will be comforted.

Hopefully the message received will be to acknowledge that there is still meaningful work to be done by you, work that can only be done by you, by no one else, work that God has assigned only to you, work that is worthwhile living to get done.

For those who neither understand what I am saying or who do not really care, I compassionately ask you to forgo this chapter until such time that you might understand or care to understand. Remember this book, *Unused Towels,* focuses on living! Many chapters offer some really funny stuff. (I especially like "Embarrassing Moments," specifically "Why I Have To Wear Sunglasses When I Shop At The Walmart In Los Lunas." Life after all *is* "a box of chocolates," or, as I prefer, a box of Assorted See's Candies.)

Also, if as you are reading this chapter and it makes no sense to you, then do yourself a favor and put it away. This is too important a topic to blather through it. Entering this mine field regarding suicide, one needs to be fully aware of the potential consequences. Believe me, suicide *is* a mine field.

Obviously prayer is important but when one is in the depths of suicidal depression, even God's unconditional love is difficult to accept. It is sometimes easier to believe that when Jesus died on the Cross it could *not* have been for *all* of our sins and that *all* of us have not been forgiven by God. For some, getting away from "What I've done is so horrible that I can't possibly be forgiven" is difficult.

Studies indicate that many of us "off" ourselves two to three months after it seemed that everything was finally going well, only to find out we've slipped back into the morass of failure. Also, most of the people who cared and helped us come out of it went away assuming (maybe hoping) that we were "okay now."

Many Others Have Written About Suicide, But ...

I've wondered should I bother writing about suicide when there are so many articles and books already written, most by so-called experts which I most often found to be absolutely worthless. Based on the surging number of suicides, apparently all the expertise published out there didn't reach the people needing help. Hopefully, some people were helped by what they read but I am personally offended that some of these "credentials" actually get published; their writings are so full of it!

My thoughts turn to wondering whether there may be one person who would benefit from reading my thoughts. Maybe one life can be saved? So please allow me to continue to share my thoughts including "my escape" from suicide.

My intention in sharing this is to help those who may have thoughts that life really isn't worth living, or, that life is too complicated – that everything goes the wrong way no matter what you do, especially if you have just gotten into a positive mindset and are working really hard to make good things happen, but everything keeps getting mucked up. The computer begins playing games with you or crashes. Even when you seem to get things right, something comes along and screws it up.

Articles About Suicide I Highly Recommend

Fortunately, there are a few articles that truly spoke to me.

One author's name is Therese Borchard; her article was titled "What Suicidal Depression Feels Like."

She began her article with the following paragraph: "I don't know if you've noticed, but ever since Robin Williams died, I have removed the filter from my writing that keeps me safe from jaw dropping, disappointing head gestures, and all kinds of judgments that authentic writing invites. I just don't really care anymore what people think because lives are at stake. If this brutal beast of an illness is strong enough to kill someone with the passion, determination, and genius of Robin Williams, then we must do everything we can to protect those who are more fragile. That means being brave and writing as honestly as I can on a taboo subject so few people understand, even if it means getting disapproving stares from other parents at my kids' school."

The rest of Ms. Borchard's comments are as mind-gripping and real as anything I've read. I fervently recommend googling this article; it is a brilliant assessment of what suicidal depression truly feels like.

Another publication I recommend has several contributors. One is Kelly McBride who was, among other things, an Opinion Contributor for *USA Today*. What caught my attention was a column with the headline, "Whispering About Suicide Won't Solve The Problem."

Ms. McBride refers to an article written by Ms. Laura Trujillo titled "Stepping Back from The Edge."

The article by Ms. Trujillo was introduced by Nicole Carroll, the Editor-in-Chief of *USA Today*, whose column was titled, "We Need To Talk About Suicide More." In her column she offers the following sobering statistics: "On average, there are 129 suicides each day, according to new data from the Centers for Disease Control and Prevention. And for every person who dies, about 29 more attempt it. It's the 10th leading cause of death in the United States."

Please note that for every person who dies, there were more than 29 attempts; that comes to 3,741 attempts a day. Based on other statistics, that is probably a serious undercount.

These three offerings by Ms. McBride, Ms. Carroll, and Ms. Trujillo were published in the November 28, 2018 issue of *USA Today*.

Ms. Trujillo's account of experiencing her mother's death by suicide and her own subsequent struggles with thinking about suicide are uniquely powerful, both beautiful and sad simultaneously. Not unlike a stunning red rose with brown thorns on its green stalk; the rose is not complete without the thorns.

Well worth reading! Be advised there is a "trigger warning" preceding the article which, if one is inclined to check out the article, definitely should be paid attention to. The article is 19 pages long.

A few excerpts from Ms. Trujillo's personal accounting of her experience with suicide:

"I had learned that when some people decide to kill themselves, they seem more at ease than they have in a long time, because they know that if they show any suicidal signs or too much distress others will try to talk them out of it.

There are researchers who will say that putting the onus on survivors is grossly unfair, that we need more money to understand suicide, to learn what works so we can do better.

It's a common feeling, this depression after losing someone to suicide, yet it often feels impossible to share. It's raw and scary, and sometimes it feels selfish or indulgent. My mom wasn't a child. She was 66, an adult who made her own decisions. And yet it consumed me.

I have learned as do many survivors of a family member's suicide, that I am now at risk.

How does someone go from happy to suicide? Was she truly happy or did we just miss the clues?

There were so many signs. It is easy to see them now.

While researchers say most suicides are more impulsive, my mom's seemed to have left an obvious trail. She was feeling helpless carrying blame, putting her affairs in order, giving away possessions. But it didn't look that way to any of us at the time.

Despite all the research, there still isn't a proven formula that can predict who is going to kill themselves and who won't; which interventions work for everyone or work for a while and which don't;

which words might save someone one day only to have them slip away the next. It doesn't make any sense why one person who demonstrates all the risk factors lives and another kills herself."

It took me close to 45 minutes to read Laura's wonderfully written story; this was not something with which to rush. The 45 minutes included time to wipe the tears off my hands as they had trickled down my cheeks and off my quivering chin.

When I finished reading Ms. Trujillo's words, I sat quietly, unable to do anything else.

I then tried to come back to my writing, but I could not yet deal with it; so I warmed my wife's homemade chicken and vegetable soup and ate two bowls. Mmmmmmmm, comforting. But I digress, although at the time I needed a distraction.

Following are a few other articles which I found extremely worth reading.

➢ "'If you are reading this, you should know that I am dead,' wrote a 27-year old army wife on her blog the year before she attempted to take her own life. Jessica Harp's blog post rippled through the military spouse community. 'I know what she feels like. It could have been me.' The struggles of military spouses made it to the national stage."

➤   "Why Depression Is A Silent Killer," by Caryl Stern, in *Parade Magazine*. When I recently read this article (September 2020), I assumed that it was an article written in the last year or so. As it turns out, it was published on September 28, 1997. What stood out for me were several statistics about "older Americans" who have attempted suicide. Note 1997 statistics: "an estimated 24,000 people 65 or older attempted suicide in 1995 and more than 6,000 succeeded. Though older people represent just 13 percent of the population, they account for almost 20 percent of all suicides – more than any other age group." (Were I to google these statistics in 2020 I would not be surprised that other age groups or peer groups, such as veterans, have unfortunately challenged these statistics.)

➤   The following also could have been written this year; it was written by Ms. Lynn Leight for *New Woman Magazine* in May *1986*. Her article was titled, "Suicide, The Last Taboo."

The following are excerpts from her article. (If you are a female, I heartily recommend reading this.) While Ms. Leight was conducting a "Support System For Suicide" session, she asked, "How many of you have ever contemplated suicide?" She indicates that:

"Each of the 12 women looked at me blankly, as though the thought had never crossed her mind.

Finally, one voice said, 'I have,' which was followed by a more timid, 'me, too' ... the final tally, 10 affirmative, one possible, one absolutely negative ...

... Only four women actually had devised and rehearsed their plans. Included in the planning were: the efficiency of the method; the selection of the optimal time, the place, and the setting; the rehearsal of the suicide; and the identifying of a contact person who might come to the rescue in the event of a last-minute change of mind."

➤   I am not sure where I found the following; it is three pages long and so I have excerpted the more critical parts. Unfortunately, I do not even have the name of the person who wrote it. He tells a very moving story:

"One day when I was a freshman in high school, I saw a kid from my class was walking home from school. His name was Kyle. It looked like he was carrying all of his books. I thought to myself, why would anyone bring home all his books on a Friday? ...

... I shrugged my shoulders and went on. As I was walking, I saw a bunch of kids running toward him. They ran at him, knocking all his books out of his arms and tripping him as he landed in the dirt. ... My heart went out to him. So I jogged over to him as he crawled around looking for his glasses, and I saw a tear in his eye. ...

... over the next four years Kyle and I became best friends. ...

... Kyle was valedictorian of our class. ...

... as he started his speech, he cleared his throat and began, 'graduations are a time to thank those who helped you make it through those tough years ... I am here to tell all of you that being a friend to someone is the best gift you can give them. I am going to tell you a story ... '

He said that he had planned to kill himself over the weekend. He talked of how he had cleaned out his locker so his mom wouldn't have to do it later ... He looked hard at me and gave me a smile ... He ended his speech, 'Thankfully, I was saved from doing the unspeakable. ... '

Never underestimate the power of your actions. With one small gesture, you can change a person's life ... for better or for worse. God puts us all in each other's lives to impact one another in some way. Look for God in others."

Lastly there have been many accounts of suicide attempts by people jumping off the San Francisco Bridge. One account that stood out for me was what one person remembered after surviving his jump: "A woman tourist approached him after he had been standing on the edge of the bridge contemplating jumping off the bridge. She approached him; he thought maybe she would ask if he were okay. Instead she asked him to take a photo of her and her friends. Then without even saying thank you, she took the camera and walked away chatting with her friends. He jumped. Later he said that had she done or said anything that said to him, 'You matter to me,' he would likely not have jumped." Lesson: It is basic to say to someone who is lonely or has given up, "You matter to me."

Note: I am adding the following on May 27, 2021, as something that I heartily recommend. This recommendation is based on an interview of Jon Hancock by Willie Geist. Jon Hancock is a Marine combat veteran who walked 5,800 miles across our country to "shine light on PTSD, suicide and healing." His walk was recorded in a documentary titled "Bastards' Road." The reviews of Mr. Hancock's documentary all acclaim the film with very high ratings. Without having viewed Mr. Hancock's documentary, his compassion as he was talking with Willie spoke powerfully to me, and so I confidently recommend his documentary.

At A Certain Point, "Words Do Not Matter"

Here I must emphasize that at a certain point in a person's trip down the suicide path, "words do not matter."

Words that make sense to us in the *sane* world often do not matter when we are in our *own lonely* world.

What *does* matter in both worlds is *action*. Don't just *say* "I care;" *show* that you care by your actions.

A sincere hug does more for a person than *the words*, "I care." This is likely one of the reasons why dogs or cats speak louder than words with the wag of their tail, or their bringing us a gift of a dead mouse. ☺

Please be aware that when you are dealing with someone on the suicide path, they (we) did not seek to be suicidally depressed; little things may have piled up, or guilt we learned growing up may have finally become too much. A sudden traumatic event in our lives may have thrown our center of sanity off so badly that regaining any sense of stability may have become close to impossible.

(If you are interested in a more detailed descent into suicide, please refer to the chapter, "TOSTI," which is an acronym for "The Other Side of The Ice." But again be forewarned, that chapter is even heavier to deal with than this chapter. I first wrote notes to myself 25 years ago describing my being on "The Other Side of The Ice." I still get tears when I read about that person, me 25 years ago. During TOSTI, I went down into the darkest moments in my life; there was no escape. I was consumed by suicidal depression.)

Suicide Today: The Elderly

Having witnessed my mother who died in her 80s, my dad who died at 94, and my mother-in-law who is getting ready to hit 94, I have seen firsthand the frustrations of the so-called elderly. Most upsetting to each of them was having little or no control of their lives: not being able to choose whether or not they go out to eat (a favorite activity for many elderly); being hurried in their shopping instead of being able to leisurely stroll around the store; someone else paying their bills; and not only others doing their shopping but making decisions about what was good for them and what was not.

In addition to this loss of control, the elderly are often also dealing with the loss of a spouse and increased social isolation. They become so sad and lonely that they ask God to let them join their spouse.

For all of them I hurt. I especially felt the pain my father endured as his life spiraled from the independent man who traveled wherever and whenever he wished after he recovered from Mom's death. And then he found himself relying on others for a lot of things, including simple daily contact. Since my sister and I did not live close by, he hired many "house cleaners," not necessarily to do any real house cleaning, but mostly to have company. He was happy just to have someone laugh at his stories and show respect for him as a person.

Suicide Today: Veterans

If you are at risk, please call the Suicide Prevention Line, currently 800.273.8255. If a veteran, press 1. Effective 16JUL22, you may also dial the three-digit code 988.

You are not alone in your thoughts. It is okay to find someone with whom you can talk about your feelings. Trust me, there **is** at least one person with whom you can share your state of mind; find him or her!

More likely, there are several fellow veterans who understand what you are dealing with. You are **not alone**! I promise you that you will feel more at peace with yourself and that over time, you will find that God still has a lot of work for you to do. He **is** waiting for you with a loving and caring heart; open your heart and soul to God, please. Just as you did when you were in combat, throw yourself fully into this survival.

My exit from suicide was due to being able to *share* my despair with someone. There are many veterans' groups near you who will welcome you.

As mentioned before, I also highly recommend Jon Hancock's documentary titled "Bastards' Road." This recommendation is based on an interview of Jon Hancock by Willie Geist. Jon Hancock, a Marine combat veteran, walked 5,800 miles across our country to "shine light on PTSD, suicide and healing." His walk was recorded in a documentary titled "Bastards' Road." The reviews of Mr. Hancock's documentary all acclaim the film with very high ratings. Reviews emphasize his "remarkable honesty, insight and humor. Jon's journey is uniquely positive. It's about changing the ways one relates to traumatic memories. It's about beginning the healing process." Although I have not yet viewed Mr. Hancock's documentary, his compassion as he was talking with Willie spoke powerfully to me, and so I confidently recommend his documentary to any veteran at risk. God bless each one of you!

I understand that alcoholics say, "Once an alcoholic, always an alcoholic – no matter how long one has been sober, never believe you are no longer an alcoholic – 'just a little drink?' can be the quick slide back."

The same applies to those who pass a certain point on their descent into suicide; the danger of considering suicide again is more prevalent. At these times, someone should not have a gun in the house or razor blades or possibly lethal drugs.

Suicide often happens when a person sinks under the weight of hopelessness and persistent depression. It is not just about the current circumstances but about the accumulation of negative circumstances. At that point it would not take much to coax the already depressed person to "just end it." *I can't deal with it anymore!*

If one has ever been prepared to take one's life, it should be expected that they *will always be* prepared to think about taking their life. (There is a critical distinction between *being prepared* to take one's life and *thinking* about taking one's life.) If you do not understand this, be thankful.

My last comment about suicide is the strong opinion that there is no such thing as an *impulsive suicide*. I strongly believe that all "surprise" suicides are preceded by a string of traumatic devastations in the person's life. After a while the burden becomes too heavy and there is nothing else which that person can control, except to "transition" into a hopefully better "life," hopefully with God's forgiveness. (Being in the state of "I can't control my failures" is often the trigger that to others resulted in the "surprise" suicide, but actually was just the last prod to "transitioning.")

My Slide Into Suicide

My slide into suicide began with a series of traumas when the two most important females in my life at the time deceived me. This deception led to a severe loss of trust that eventually caused me to question my very life, leading to excruciating self-doubt and acute depression.

As my slide continued, I began to lose confidence in myself about everything. Projects on which I had been working were still going well, but I began to feel that they were going well without me, and perhaps in spite of me.

From there just about everything seemed to go downhill ... usually only in my mind, not in reality ... but it is difficult to acknowledge the difference once one is regressing.

Eventually, an overwhelming emotion surfaced that I could never trust another woman again. (Were I a female, the emotion could easily have been "I'll never trust another man again;" gender was not the critical factor.) From there, the slide into depression became steeper with no realistic hope of escape.

All that was left was a series of debilitating self-doubts: *What is it that I want to escape? I really don't want to live any longer. I have no reason to live, no one to live for. I prayed for God to help me find a reason that made sense to live; I heard no response ... even God wanted to have nothing to do with me.*

My dad joined in and criticized me for not being able to deal with my marriage. He did not know that my ex had lied to me and cheated on me while we were married.

The slide continued: "I've disappointed my kids."

I was clearly not important to anyone. I was not special to anyone. I kept doing lots of things for lots of people but no one in my life made me care. I began to believe that the projects I was working on were not likely to result in successes. I thought, "If I knew how to end my life *for sure* tonight, I would; but I would probably screw that up too."

On 6Feb93/0800, I started to write a lengthy draft for an article, "Thoughts In Preparation For Taking My Life."

The draft began:

> "By the end of this month, I intend to take my life, or in words which I prefer, 'to transition to another life.'"

I continued,

> "Taking my life is *not* what I wish to do. It is the only action, however, which I believe will rid me of my constant headaches (unusual for me) and my physically stressed body.

It is the only action I feel I can control.

Healing my hurts has not worked. Ceasing to be a disappointment to certain people who were very important in my life hasn't happened. Correcting my life seems impossible."

Fifteen pages later, the draft ended with the following words written on 19Feb93/9:00pm:

"I have nothing else to add. Instead, I cry every time I read my words. *I wish I were someone else* so that I could hold me, love me, look into my eyes and feel my hurt. Then, I believe *I could* love me and give me a reason to want to live and love."

It's tough. I lost all ability to feel love. I lost any confidence that anyone *truly* cared about me. I felt like no one could understand how I felt since I did not understand how I felt, or why I felt the way I felt.

A person could "off" himself in a moment of emotional distress – anger at their spouse/loved one who is a downer and who blames them! "If I had a gun right now, I would consider using it."

I asked myself, "On a scale of 0-10 how offended would God be if I took my life? Am I meaningful to His much larger scheme of the universe and creating man in His image? What is one less useless soul?"

Other questions followed: "How much would I hurt others? Who would I hurt? Would they actually be relieved not to have to deal with my mood swings? How many more things am I going to mess up if I stay alive?" (At the time of my deepest suicidal depression, the O. J. Simpson trial was on television from dawn to dusk. That kept me distracted during the weekdays. Weekends were hell without any distractions and worse, with friends calling me to get together.)

My Exit (For Now) From Suicide

My exit from suicide was not due to any effort on my part. It certainly was not due to prayers since months earlier I had begun to talk to God as though He were my enemy. Certainly He was not someone who I believed was interested in helping me. I am amazed that God did not strike me with lightening for the disrespectful ways I talked to Him.

Alas, God never deserted me. Even while I was busy cussing at Him, He continued to stand behind me, with a tear in His eye, quietly saying, *"I am here. Trust that I am here and know that I love you unconditionally."*

And then ...

God sent me four angels; each one helped nudge me up from the deep slide I had fallen into. These angels were sent to me at the lowest points in my life. Two of them were sent as I was in the final steps, just before "the transition."

The first angel called as I was ready to take my last step. I had visited her at her insistence the weekend before. She was calling me with tears in her voice. Her brother having taken his life a year earlier and her sister-in-law having recently died, she was in a very delicate state of mind and must have picked up hints that maybe I was also on the brink of taking my own life.

In this case, she did not do a lot of listening as she was pleading with me not to do what her younger brother had done a year earlier, unexpectedly take his life. "I can't lose you too." Out of respect for her I compromised with my inclination and the thought, "Okay, not today." And so, "not today" eventually turned into "not this month," over and over.

The second angel popped into my life in such a way that it had to be a miracle. The call came from a posh art gallery on Rodeo Drive in Beverly Hills. I was living in Tucson at the time. A call from Beverly Hills?

Part of the reason why I attribute this entire experience with my second angel to be a miracle is that for some unknown reason I answered the phone, something I had not done for several weeks.

Although I was a bit busy at the time, I put down the razor blade to pick up the telephone.

The voice on the other end said, "Hi, I'm Amy P. I'm calling you from "xyz Art Gallery" in Beverly Hills. You were here last summer and expressed interest in the LeRoy Neiman elephant painting, 'Elephant Charge.' I'm sorry that we have not called you since you were here in June but ..."

The voice suddenly stopped talking and she said, "You're not okay, are you?"

I burst into tears.

Amy listened and cared.

This whole series of unbelievable events with my second angel began when my oldest daughter invited my ex's daughter to come visit her for a week in Los Angeles. My ex agreed but, for some unexplainable reason, only on the condition that I take her daughter to LA.

When we arrived in LA, my daughter asked "The Bean" what she would like to do while she was there. HB being a wonderfully precocious 13-year-old immediately said, "Go shopping on Rodeo Drive."

And so there we were walking down Rodeo Drive when we passed a window with paintings by LeRoy Neiman. One riveting painting in the middle of the display was his "Elephant Charge." Having admired his work, I stopped and suggested we go in.

For another unexplainable reason, the owner approached us and after talking with us briefly invited us into a private viewing room where he brought in several paintings, one being the "Elephant Charge." When asked if I were interested, I said something about how terrific it was but knowing that there was no way I could afford it, I mentioned having a friend in San Diego who also liked elephants. I knew that she could afford it for her condo in La Jolla. I took his card and apparently left my name and Tucson telephone number with him.

Five months later, the phone rang and I found myself talking with Amy, a total stranger, who had called me from the art gallery. Curiously, the visit to the art gallery had occurred back in June; it was now November. My being on Rodeo Drive for the first and only time in my life was already extraordinary. And now a phone call? Why the phone call at this moment?

Amy, not knowing me, was genuinely concerned for me. She cared enough to forego the sale of the painting ... the original purpose of her call, and instead focused on me. From 500 miles away, she had the ability to *feel* over the phone a stranger's hurt and struggles.

Over the next few months, Amy and I developed a human-caring relationship that steered me to put away all my razor blades for a long time and instead to focus on living rather than on "transitioning."

Years later, I again slowly slipped back into full despair. During this time, I met a woman about my father's age who "guided" me to my third angel. I do not recall the specific circumstances under which I met this woman, nor do I recall *why* or *what* I said to her that moved her to suggest that I see G. N., a kinesiologist, who turned out to be my third angel. I had never heard of a kinesiologist but, once again, I was inexplicably guided to call her for an appointment. G. N. not only helped stabilize me over time but became a good friend of mine (as well as a friend of the fourth angel who God sent me).

The fourth angel I had met twenty years earlier in Kansas. Now I was in Arizona and she was in California. When we met earlier she was married and I was with the woman with whom I thought I would spend the rest of my life. As the years went by, we both moved several times and became single. For again some reason only God was privy to, we exchanged birthday cards every year, and thus we kept in touch with one another.

Over time, we refreshed our friendship, eventually she becoming my Mary of whom one can read in many of these chapters. Mary and I celebrated our twentieth wedding anniversary last year. She is my pillar now; brought together by God in another unbelievable miracle.

As one can see, my slide out of suicide was due to a series of random actions: my daughter inviting my ex-wife's daughter to visit her in LA; my ex-wife agreeing but on the condition that I take her daughter to LA; HB choosing to go shopping on Rodeo Drive; LeRoy Neiman's "Elephant Charge" on display at an expensive Beverly Hills Gallery; the owner taking us into one of the private viewing rooms to more closely look at the painting; my giving him my name and telephone number; one of his staff, Amy, calling me *five months later*, my putting down the razor blade I had in my hand to answer the telephone after weeks of not answering the phone for *any* reason; Amy *sensing* over the telephone that I was not okay and *showing* that she cared; my Mary sending me birthday cards for over 25 years after we had met in Kansas, both of us moving several times; Mary's agreeing to help me with my business thus bringing us more in touch with one another;

our miracle experience at the *Santuario de Chimayo* in Chimayo, New Mexico.

I am sure these are just the tips of several icebergs; there are undoubtedly thousands of other random actions that God performed over the years that eventually ended with my exiting out of suicidal thoughts.

Nonetheless, there was a reason why I qualified my "Exit (For Now) From Suicide" with the words "For Now." I am fully aware that like an alcoholic, once someone passes a certain point on the path to taking one's own life, one must remain ever vigilant for any degree of depression and remember that like an alcoholic, "just a little drink" could cause the slide again.

If this is difficult for you to understand, then I am glad for you. That may mean that you are fortunate enough to exist in a world where neither you nor someone dear to you is struggling with suicidal thoughts.

I conclude this chapter with a sincere and affectionate message:

Sometimes the pain does not go away; you *have* to grow around it.

Look for God in others; that little bit of trust in God can make a major difference in one's life.

Even when things seem to be going well, and something messes it up, *remember* that it is important to never give up. There is yet important work to be done by you, work that no one else can do! Remember Kyle.

Keep in mind that words without action don't mean a lot. If you can, show that you care by wagging your tail, or bringing a gift of a dead mouse to the one about whom you care. ☺

God bless you and remember you *are* important to many people, including me. ☺

Remember that God is always looking over our shoulders, and although His answers to our prayers are not necessarily the answers we want, they are very likely the better answers.

God's reminder that "It works better when we do it together" is a tried and true path. Bottom line: Bring God into your life, your struggles, your failures, your successes, your projects, concerns, or obstacles.

Lastly, remember:

"Let trust in God control you,"

&

"In All Things Give Thanks, For This Is The

Will Of God Concerning

You."

1 Thessalonians 5:18

Teacher,
A Very Special Second Grade Teacher,
My Son

(Beach Towel)

Thirty years ago, I spent a very special day in my son's classroom when he was teaching second grade.

Living across the country, my visits were limited in time. However, when my son invited me to come along and spend the day in his second grade classroom, I gladly accepted the invitation.

Immediately upon walking into his classroom, I noticed that everything about how he conducted his classes was something I had never experienced.

First, the classroom was set up to reinforce *working with others* (as independent of the teacher as practicable). The students were not sitting in a line of desks. Instead they were seated at little round tables with four or five students at each table, facing one another.

After "Mr. C" set the objectives for the day and explained any unspecified details, the students were ready to take charge, working with one another to accomplish the day's objectives.

As I observed Mr. C during the day, there was another very important difference in how he made the day's assignments seem more like a series of projects, much more exciting and enjoyable than working on "homework-type" tasks. Every lesson was one that each student would be able to actually use at the end of the day, something which had a clear function ... not something that merely was to be memorized and rarely used in real life like so much of what I had been taught in my elementary classes.

Walking amongst them, "just being there" should any of the students have questions, he remained a "go-to" advisor if they got stuck. Once in a while I also observed a group discussing ideas on how to accomplish the task in an improved manner from what Mr. C had outlined. After calling him over to discuss their thoughts and receiving an encouraging response, the group would move on, sometimes excitedly stopping to share with other tables their "new and improved" way of proceeding.

A gleeful yell would often follow their distinctive pride at coming up with an even better solution. (I found out after class that Mr. C often did that purposely thus encouraging the students to always look for a better way of accomplishing the task.)

I also observed that as the day went on, there was no separation by gender; there was no distinction between what little girls "were supposed to do," versus, what little boys were expected to do. (This was back in the 1990s, long before society caught up with fully appreciating the skills and talents that females have. Many adult executive secretaries were still making coffee for their bosses, just because they were a female, and then hurrying back to get their own work done.)

❖

One of the most memorable observations highlighted Mr. C's method of "just being there," as their go-to advisor if they got stuck.

This being the Friday before Father's Day, each child had been told to bring a photograph of themselves with which to make their Father's Day cards. If they came from a divorced family, they were encouraged to bring two photographs so that they could create a card for their step-father and one for their biological father.

One little girl suddenly became frustrated because she had "messed up" one of her Father's Day cards. One boy, bigger than the other kids, began loudly pestering her about how she had messed up.

As the little girl became irritated at the boy, who even in second grade outweighed her by a good 20 pounds, to my surprise Mr. C. did nothing.

Instead he sat back and watched as every single student in that classroom immediately walked over to her table and turned their backs on the bully.

They next began to discuss how she could salvage the card on which she had glued her photograph upside down. All the other artwork had been completed taking several hours and therefore could not realistically be corrected.

As the group focused on helping the little girl, ignoring their own work, one student came up with the idea that she could add words and graphics to her card in order to make it into "a silly card."

The little girl became excited at this solution and told the other children that one of her father's pet names for her was "silly girl."

It was a perfect solution. The students then went back to their own tables, proudly congratulating one another. I also overheard one student say that he was going to change his Father's Day card into a "silly card."

This story does not end there.

About fifteen minutes later, I looked over at an unbelievable sight. The bully had walked over to the little girl to ask her for help with *his* cards.

She took him by the hand and they walked back across the room to his table.

It was quite a sight!

The little girl bringing along the boy who not only outweighed but was three or four inches taller than her. He was following her like a little puppy.

Beautiful!

❖

At the end of this day, I thought about what I had experienced for the first time in my life, *in my 40s:*

First, the classroom was set up to encourage working together.

Second, the teacher had developed a fine line between being a teacher and being a coach, resulting in what I would describe as a mentor. (An experienced and trusted advisor who advises, provides guidance, gives feedback and lends support). The result was that the students *knew* they were trusted to work out problems with one another if at all possible. This environment set the path to celebrate *their* accomplishments in "gleeful shouts," a new experience for me, since

I do not recall ever hearing anything resembling "a gleeful yell" in any of my classes. Instead the typical monotonic words heard in my grade school classes were, "Quiet children," "Yes, Sister D," "No Mrs. Glum," "Yes, Mr. Dixon."

Finally and most importantly, the students ...

... I observed second-grade students, *very young adults*, with enough confidence in themselves and in working with others that it was "natural" to challenge themselves to find a better direction, to be unafraid to *respectfully* question the teacher, to be fully confident in going a different direction. A subtle outcome of this self-confidence resulted in the students addressing the problems in creative ways, not limiting themselves to the "stated problem," i.e., their solution to what was realistically an almost unsolvable problem (the graphics of the little girl's card with the glued upside-down photo). They instead chose to ignore the glued-upside photo as an error and transformed the solution by adding a different dimension to the card, *the creation* of a "silly card for Daddy's Little Silly Girl."

It was especially admirable that the kids banded together to put the bully in his place. Too often bullies get away with their bullying as other kids join in on the bullying because they want to be liked, or they are afraid of the bully turning on them. These kids instinctively knew how to come to the aid of the person being bullied and simultaneously letting the bully know in no uncertain terms that it was he who was being shut out.

After that day, I often told my son, "I wish I'd had a teacher like you when I was in second grade; my life would have been so different since I did not develop the level of self-confidence that you taught your second-grade kids until I was thirty years old."

◆ ◆ ◆

Prior to this experience in his classroom, the "other story" about my son was one I had cherished most as the one experience to *always remember,* a hike with him to the bottom of the Grand Canyon, enhanced by two nights of indescribable camping by the banks of the Colorado River. However, this dream-of-a-lifetime experience at the Grand Canyon now *paled* in comparison to this one very special day observing "my son, the teacher and his students."

(For most fathers, this Grand Canyon experience would most likely be the father-son union to always remember; I cannot imagine any son who would not cherish such a connection either.)

This Grand Canyon experience had occurred five years earlier when my son came out to visit me for the summer in San Diego. We had what was truly one of those once-in-a-lifetime experiences. We hiked the Grand Canyon spending two nights camped at the Bright Angel

Campground sleeping so close to the Bright Angel Creek that we could hear the babbling, gurgling sounds of the creek water just before it flowed into the Colorado River.

This happened the first summer that he came to visit me for the summer. When I asked if there were anything special he wanted to do, he said, "Yes, can we hike the Grand Canyon?"

I blurted out, "Sure, but I'm going to have to get into shape."

As we talked, his excitement grew greater when we pondered the option of spending the night at the campsite by the Colorado River.

We agreed that I would begin a regimen of hiking so that I could be ready by the end of the summer to do the long hike out of the Canyon. He was in his teens and I was in my 30s.

As it turned out, camping passes were not available until near the end of the summer anyway.

When the day arrived, after work just before dusk, we climbed into my little black Nissan Sentra, "Fury," pulled back the moon roof and took off for the Grand Canyon from San Diego.

The drive itself was special, laying back the passenger seat so one could look straight up gazing out the moon roof and seeing the night sky full of sparkling white stars as we drove though the darkened deserts of California and Arizona, arriving at the Grand Canyon a few hours before dawn.

We got a few more hours of rest, and then we checked in, got our hiking permits and overnight camping passes.

The hike down the Canyon was relaxing and enjoyable.

When we arrived at the banks of the Colorado River, we stopped and took in the amazing sights and sounds of being at the bottom of the Grand Canyon.

We then crossed the river, checked in at the National Park Service office (NPS) and located our reserved camp-site.

Sleeping next to the babbling Bright Angel Creek which empties into the Colorado River! Seeing the stars against a clear dark sky! Waking in the morning to the sunrise over the rim of the canyon. The days and nights at the bottom of the Canyon were special in so many ways.

The time went by too quickly, as though in a dream. I took magazine-worthy pictures of him rinsing his short brown hair in the creek, catching individual droplets of water as he shook the water off his head. At night we listened to the silence of the natural scene, hearing only the native animals and the babbling, gurgling sounds of the creek water just before it flowed into the Colorado River. Sleeping more soundly than at any other time in my life, I recall with a measure of enjoyment as I was awakened by a small mouse scampering across my sleeping bag. A wonderful little BF. ☺

This was a trip *for the ages*, one old guy and his young, body-building son.

On the last morning he had wanted to be the first ones to hike out that morning so we took off by the light of a full moon. We were the first "civilians" to make it out of the canyon although one of the NPS staff whizzed by us as we neared the top. When I said, "Oh no, my son wanted to be the first ones out," she pointed out that she was not carrying camping supplies weighing 30-40 pounds, adding that she was one of the staff and she had hiked out of the canyon over a hundred times.

At the rim we showered and then went to eat at the El Tovar Restaurant where we feasted on steak and eggs. When he was through with his steak, something told me he was still hungry. When I offered a second steak and eggs, his eyes popped up and he said, "Are you sure? Did you see what it costs?"

The cost of the steaks did not begin to compare with the value of that experience ...

... an experience which later was surpassed by that one day in my son's second grade classroom!

Thots, Random

(Beach Towel)

The Day I Used Duct Tape To Fix An Old Pair Of Slippers

In the spirit of my Mary who does not preach at me but importantly inspires me, I watched with a slight sense of horror at what I had wrought with my old slippers.

That was the day I used duct tape to fix an old pair of slippers.

It could not be? Was this another sign of an ART (ART – Age Related Thing)? Omygosh!

I quickly looked down to see if I were wearing white socks with sandals! I was not! Nor was I wearing a white belt with dark pants. No suspenders either!

[Regarding ART – Age Related Thing - I just made up this acronym. If it previously existed, please pardon me for claiming it; when I googled it, I found it not. It is actually borrowed from my 90-year-old mother-in-law who loves to refer to ARIs (Age Related Incidents or Issues) as reasons for her behavior. I like ART better.]

But back to duct taping my favorite and *really comfortable* slippers.

Sure, they were slightly battered, a hole in the sole and two in the heel, but they weren't BIG holes, at least not *really big*; a "3x5" card easily covered each one of the holes ... ☺ ... and besides, who's going to see the duct tape in the privacy of my own home?

Besides, my Mary will likely beam at what I have learned from her.

Interestingly, Mary did not grow up poor – not rich but certainly rich enough to buy duct tape, something which my family could not afford. [Confession: duct tape had not been invented when I was a kid. ☺]

And here I am today, able to afford new slippers. I believe I even have two or three useable pair, one of them in an unopened box. The other two do not need *fixing* but I just did not care about them for one reason or another.

Instead, I find myself using duct tape to fix my slippers. (Wow, I *am* suffering through an ART!) Although I must admit that the duct tape fix did not work particularly well; I had to keep adding new tape every few days. Thus, I feel reasonably confident that I will not repeat that particular ART.

Thanks To *The New York Times Magazine* For Not Suing Me
For Not Getting Permission
To Quote Some Beautiful Thoughts From Their Pages

The following two "random thots" are copied from the December 15, 2019 issue of *The New York Times Magazine*; no permission asked. Were I to believe that this (my) page would receive world-wide attention or fame, I would certainly call and ask for permission to quote these, but I really doubt that I am doing anything so famous as to render this illegal or immoral. But, "if it should come to pass," please excuse me and call my attorney (*if* I had one).

On page 12, from various letters from folks who were moved by an article from the December 1 issue in "The Thread:" words from LL, Kansas City: "These stories mirror my own 63 years, with all the ups and downs that every person experiences. Because of this series, I became a documentary professional ... thank you for taking us with you on this journey called life. I am eternally grateful."

Related to the same article, words from Mary from Decatur Ga: " ... things change and things end. But, oh, I loved the dance with these people."

And lastly, from MW, Athens, Ga: " ... encapsulates the complex tangle of emotions and desires every parent must feel when they look at their children. Thank you for writing this."

Thank you, LL, Mary and MW. Your comments about something you have read give me optimism that my words in my book, *Unused*

Towels, may make others feel about my writings as you did about the article you read. I especially loved the vision in my head from Mary from Decatur, " ... But, oh, I loved the dance with these people." (I believe these three comments were about a Gideon Lewis-Kraus article regarding someone named Michael Apted. My apologies to both of you; I am not familiar with you, but you obviously affected many as described by these three lovely souls.)

Also, from the same December 15, 2019 issue of *The New York Times Magazine*, again, no permission asked: this one is about a poem selected by Noomi Shihab Nye: "Memory permeates awareness again and again, illuminating the absent, suggesting not that we keep it alive but that it may keep us alive."

Thank you, *The New York Times Magazine*, and please be not upset with me. These are such wonderful commentaries on the value your readers find in your writings; I'm sure you don't mind sharing them with folks.

... And Then This Happened

One Sunday evening, my wife and I decided to check out a laid-back brewery, the Kaktus Brewery, in the neighboring town of Bernalillo, a quaint little 100-plus year-old town.

The brewery has a unique setting, clearly worthwhile checking out.

One of our servers was a sweet, clearly intelligent young lady named Natalie. (She appeared to be in her 20s.) In the "laid-backness" of the place, there was a lot of conversation among customers and staff, most of whom it appeared had met that evening.

Sensing that Natalie's being a server was only a make-money-stopping-point (with which Mary and I could easily relate), we began talking with her about our mutual lives, including what she wanted to be when she "grew up." Natalie cheerily sat down and reiterated the sense that she had much bigger plans than being a server the rest of her life [" ... not that there's anything wrong with that!" (Thanks, Seinfeld!)]

As she started to tell us about her well-thought out plans, she sweetly, without complaining, pointed to her obviously pregnant stomach and said, "... and then this happened," clearly suggesting that because of that, her plans were on-hold. Again, no complaints, "just the facts."

I mention Natalie since I could relate to her situation in that I had to deal with "... and then this happened" in my own life (not 'pregnant' of course ☺). However, I did not respond in the optimistic way that Natalie had. With her positive attitude, Natalie will possibly be the owner and co-founder of a string of restaurants, or, perhaps a scientist who discovers some to-this-day unknown drug. Whatever she accomplishes will definitely be something along those lines.

To remind myself of Natalie and her attitude, I have made myself a poster with the words: " ... and then this happened."

In the past, when I was confronted with " ... and then this happened," I found myself "stopped," and not able to move forward. It was not always a full stop but more of a squirrelly wiggling wobble, not going anywhere at the pace and with the energy with which I started. Sometimes I have used that as an excuse for quitting and not pursuing my plans. Or at best, as an explanation for changing my plans, ignoring that my original plans were in fact good plans, just needing some time and thought to get past the obstacle. I cannot count the number of times I have done that. One of my weaknesses is that I succumb to "giving up" so easily. It often takes a major effort or kick in the butt for me not to do so.

Thank you, Natalie for helping me to continue to learn.

Words Inside The Cover Of A CD

I just love the simplicity of these words:

Reflect like a mirror

Respond like an echo

Healing touch

Opening

Near and far away

Slow voyage

Clear pools

Native pulse

Speaking in tongues

Rousseau's jungle

The title of the CD is "reflect like a mirror, respond like an echo." The artist: a produce. The CD was originally made by Trance Port in Los Angeles in 1992. There was a re-release in 1997. My copy is the 1992 product.

Let This Be About The Emergence Of The Exceptional Self!

From Lazaris, Los Angeles, March 20, 1992: " ... filled with inner-knowing, filled with self-doubt, you wonder if you dare cross, dare to begin. At the crest of that bridge, someone stands ready to gently take you by the hand and guide you, ready to give you the courage to cross into – to invade – your own privacy. This one can make it safe. This one is the exceptional self."

MUs or OPs

When I cannot seem to get motivated to do something and I find the task overwhelming and I struggle for direction to get going, I often spend an undue amount of time getting started, procrastinating endlessly. One solution I have found is to break the task into "Manageable Units" (MUs) or "Observable Progress" (OPs).

Breaking the task down into MUs or OPs gives me permission to know that I do not have to finish the entire task immediately. All I need to do is just get something worthwhile accomplished. Sort of like knowing that I do not have to score a touchdown on each play, but that it is important to advance the ball enough to get a "First and Ten" in four downs. This is much more realistic and surprisingly *do-able!* Usually before I know it, I have completed what I once felt was overwhelming.

All The Staples And Paper Clips I'll Ever Need

It is concurrently freeing and a bit melancholic to know that I have enough staples and paper clips to last me the rest of my life.

The genesis of this lament is our supply cabinet in which Mary and I have left-over supplies from our business days of producing class room materials and workshop handouts. Although we have made several deliveries of 3-ring binders, art supplies, pens and pencils and various other many-and-sundry supplies to an elementary school near our house, we nonetheless kept enough such that we need not worry about running out of many of the basic office supplies.

This thought will likely *not* be understood by those not yet approaching the last years of their lives ... and who knows, the Good Lord may choose to keep me around for another 15-20 years; so I better watch our use of staples and not waste ... Ha!

Another concern with which we no longer live is that there is plenty of recycle paper for the printer as well as for scratch paper for notes and such.

Waste not, want not!

One-Liners Dribbling Out Of My Pencil

[My apologies to the initial sources for much of the material that follows. These are inspirational or witty one-liners which I have been jotting down for over forty years. Whenever I heard something that inspired me, I wrote it down. I never intended to include these in any writings, and therefore I did not need to record the initial source of these wisdoms nor write the exact words.]

An example of one of the thoughts I wrote down over 40 years ago and have carried with me came from one of the greatest persons I ever worked with, Gerry M. (One of the two highlights of my professional career!) Although Gerry swears he does not remember saying the following, I *know* he said it over 40 years ago when we worked together in Scottsdale: "The oxen are slow, but the earth is patient." (Gerry, that was such a creative thought that inspired me many, many times over my life. Thanks, and I *am* sure *you* said it!!)

As I said, many of the "one-liners" have been slightly altered to better relate to my circumstances and needs. "The oxen are slow, but the earth is patient" is one fine example. My alteration rings true for me way more often than it should. To wit: "I am slow, but God is patient."

Likewise many of the one-liners which follow have been slightly altered. Please feel free to do likewise; alter any of these to better suit your desires. ☺

I believe the following first saw the light as they dribbled out of my pencil, in one way or another, inspiring or humoring me:

> God provides food for the birds but He doesn't throw it in their nests.

> Pray as though everything depends on God *and* work as though everything depends on you.

> If you wanna rest … try planned laziness … no regrets, no guilt feelings!   (You are actually being productive; you are accomplishing something which you set out to do. Eh?)

- Appreciate your own God-loaned talents.

- Channel those skills and talents that are "just lying around." We all have them! Use 'em. They ain't gonna do nobody no good if they just sit around.

- Feel their souls; feed your soul!

- A little distraction is okay, for example, watching TV, unless it becomes your imaginary friend for long periods of time.

- It's a much happier world when you're clueless.

- Remember that you are one of a kind! If you don't believe this, just ask God when you see Him/Her how many more like you there are.

- The talents God has loaned me are mine alone; should I not have used them when I die, they do not pass on to anyone else! The old maxim, "Use it or lose it" could not be more true than in this regard.

- "The honeymoon is over!" ☺ (This is a phrase that my angel and I "moan" to one another when either of us feels that we are not getting the attention desired.)

- "The honeymoon continues!" (This is the trailing phrase my angel and I "smile" to one another when we are given the correct amount of attention desired.)

- Originally from Max Lucado: "God has given us all the reservoirs and talents that we need to fulfill our mission on this earth. Our mission is *our* mission, no one else's. Trust God on this."

My addition: "God did not intend for us to contest the talents of Albert Einstein, or Anne Frank, or Thomas Edison, or Georgia O'Keeffe, or Marie and Louis Pasteur, or Martin Luther King, or Malala Yousafzal, or Mother Mary Teresa Bojaxhiu, or Maya Angelou, or Michelangelo di Lodovico Buonarroti Simoni, or Rosa Parks, or Sojourner Truth, or (add one of your favorite persons). So, be the best you can be! You are the only you! When you die, there will be no one continuing to be you." And from Ralph Waldo Emerson: "the only person you are destined to become is the person you decide to be."

➢ Be concise. Get to the point within 30 seconds.

➢ To increase the chances of something being remembered say it in a series of three; change words slightly but not the meaning.

➢ If something needs to be changed, do it quickly.

➢ Before a job interview, remember that you will not be hired based on one capability.

One-Liners Dribbling Out Of Someone Else's Pencil

From other's minds or pencils ... sorry, I have no source to identify most. Sometimes I have made minor modifications to make them more relevant to me:

"I'm not upset that you lied to me. I'm upset that from now on I can't trust you."
Friedrich Neitzsche

"Unless you fell on your treadmill, no one wants to hear about your workout."
Source Unknown

"Your arms are too short to box with God."
Source Unknown

"Dear Vegans: If you are trying to save the animals, stop eating their food."
Source Unknown

"Astronomers have found that the universe is expanding faster than people care."
Demetri Martin, (American Airlines) American Way

"Don't believe everything you think."
(From Hem's journey in Out of the Maze.)

"What if soy milk is just regular milk introducing itself to you in Spanish, 'Ola, soy milk.'" [Translation into English: "Hi, I'm milk."]
Source Unknown

"Every year global warming is responsible for the destruction of more than 10,000 dinner conversations."
Demetri Martin, (American Airlines) American Way

"Zoologists have found that after an animal is placed on the endangered species list, it tends to 'act more cocky.'"
Demetri Martin, (American Airlines) American Way

"What is there that I have been too lazy or too busy to pursue, caress, investigate, or improve?"
Source Unknown

"Anything I say before my first cup of coffee cannot be used against me."
Source Unknown

"Continue to connect with your curiosity now, or, maybe even with curiosities taken away from you as a child or maybe even as an adult. For example:

How did that flower get there?

Why is the sky blue?

What did it mean that God created the world in seven days?

What will I ask God first when I get to heaven? What will be my next question?

If I ask God can I hug Him/Her, will He/She say yes?"
Source Unknown

"Is God a "He, or, a She, or, maybe just God?" (I like this last one best.)"
Source Unknown

"It's important to let them know they are loved, that they are important."
Source Unknown

"Studies have shown that it is physically impossible to look cool while chasing a piece of paper down a windy street."
Demetri Martin, (American Airlines) American Way

"I've learned that opportunities are never lost; someone will take the ones you miss."
Source Unknown

"I've learned that I wish I could have told my Mom that I loved her one more time before she passed away."
Source Unknown

"I've learned that one should keep one's words both soft and tender, because tomorrow I may have to eat them."
   Source Unknown

"I've learned that a smile is an inexpensive way to improve my looks."
   Source Unknown

"Remember that successful people are 'a dime-a-dozen.'"
   Source Unknown

"Let go of whatever isn't working."
   (From Hem's journey in Out of the Maze.)

"Never lend books – nobody ever returns them; the only books I have in my library are those which people have lent me."
   Anatole France

"Great minds discuss ideas; Average minds discuss events; Small minds discuss people."
   Eleanor Roosevelt

"Remember" Versus "Don't Forget"

This is another one of those *really random* thots. When I remind myself to "Remember," it is a positive action that I am encouraging.

Although a subtle difference, when told "Don't forget," I feel almost chastised since I am being told to make sure I do not take a negative action, "*Don't* do ..."

Subtle yes, but I enjoy being encouraged to *do* something, rather than being discouraged.

Subtle differences, but then, are we not subtle creatures? ☺

Thots, Random – My Baby's

(Wash Cloth)

Titles Of Books Mary Wants To Write

"Sunglasses in the Rain"

"As Soon As I Finish Kicking Myself"

"The Day I Had To Ride The Broom"

Mary's Magical Maxims

" ... I'm sorry but that is my point of reference."

"... that's my story and I stand uncorrected!"

"... thoughts keep falling out of my mouth ... don't pay attention to me."

... giving birth to "get even cake."

... giving birth to "I did it for you cake," aka, "I ate it for you cake."

... "wishful hearing!"

... "opposite hearing!"

... "sometimes when I'm thinking, I'm not listening!"

... "I'm going to step out of my mind for a minute."

... "may I step into your mind for a minute?"

After 20 years of marriage, my wife suddenly asked me, "If I pull your finger, will you fart for me?"

Mary's favorite flavor of ice cream: "More!"

The following is not so much a "maxim," but a typical "I have no idea why I said that" from Mary:

> At a reception for Garrison Keillor which we were fortunate to attend, we waited for the crowd to dissipate until we were the only two non-staff left in the room. Mr. Keillor graciously noticed and came over to us when we gushed about how much we had enjoyed his performance.

For some reason, Mary went on to tell him that her father really enjoyed his radio shows, "My father found you hilarious. Being a Lutheran, he especially appreciated the references to 'Our Lady of Perpetual Guilt' Church."

Mary then made a comment about political persuasions. Keillor replied, "So, he was a Republican?"

Mary answered, "Well, he was a registered 'Republican' but … my Dad would often tease and refer to 'mugwumps,' those who have their 'mugs' on one side of the fence and their 'wumps' on the other."

Keillor looked at her with curiosity and then graciously accepted the earlier compliment and was in the process of leaving when Mary blurted out, "I hope you'll keep practicing!"

He stopped, looked back at her with those famous, furled, bushy eyebrows, and then he walked away.

I told Mary that I knew that she was complimenting him with a flattering "keep up the good work," but instead, the look on his face suggested that perhaps he thought she was telling him, "Keep practicing; someday you'll get it right."

I would not be surprised if that incident made it into his next performance. ☺

Thots, Tidbits

(Wash Cloth)

The following are a few thoughts that could easily go into a chapter titled "Miscellaneous." However, I fear that such a title would not be particularly inviting to any reader when in fact there is much more than random "miscellany" here. However, these are thoughts that did not merit being in other chapters. Each tidbit is short; something to read while waiting for the microwave to beep.

Tidbits Escaping From My Mind

One of my best received speeches was to a room full of beautifully gray and white haired ladies. The State Toastmistress Governor had heard a speech of mine at a Toastmaster's contest titled, "Elephants, Belly Buttons, Love Affairs and Other Helpful Hints."

When she invited me to be a speaker at their state convention, she asked me to give the same speech with no changes. As it turned out, their convention was being held at one of the retirement communities in the Phoenix area and therefore the majority in attendance were "locals," residents of the retirement community.

The speech was not about having romantic affairs but it was replete with suggestions for having a romantic affair ... *with life*. Of course, there were various overt innuendos that aroused quiet giggles every now and then.

I don't recall the details of the speech; the speech itself is not the point. What is memorable for me is that I can still see the inquisitive, sparkling eyes from every gorgeous face in the room. (Not that it is particularly relevant, but I was in my 30's at the time.)

Even though the speech was not sexual in nature, it was romantic enough that I remember a standing ovation. (When one is not accustomed to standing ovations, one tends to remember the rare ones.)

Besides the standing ovation, I remember that experience *now* when I start feeling too old and I am reminded by those glistening eyes that life is not over until we choose to exit. (I just saw an 85-year old woman on "The Price is Right" run up on stage and plant a big old smooch on Drew Carey's face. "Yeah!" for not checking out of life while there is still breath inside our little souls and minds.) The body may be straining for breath but the soul and mind do not expire until we give up. As *they* say, "God did not place automatic expiration dates on us." Some of us do that ourselves. I remind myself that I still have work to do, work that no one else will do if I do not take care of it myself. No *unused towels* left behind, nor any God-loaned talents and skills left behind!

Secondly, I wish to express a long-felt, never adequately verbalized, appreciation to the *Chicago Tribune* which during the Vietnam War offered free subscriptions to "US Forces stationed overseas." It was uplifting to find out what was going on "back home," even if the news was weeks-old; the mail planes came in from McGuire AFB only when the weather permitted so sometimes there would be two or three weeks worth of news. I also deeply appreciated that great performer, Sammy Davis Jr., and the USO for bringing him to entertain us – *that* was special!

Tidbits Escaping From Other People's Minds

"In all things, give thanks for this is the will of God concerning you."
1 Thessalonians 5:18 (God)

"What people do not understand does not exist."
1986 Not Just Another Publishing Company

"Fuzzy goals usually produce fuzzy results."
(Author unknown)

"It's past time for action; it's time for senseless bickering!"
(Author unknown)

"Long term planning for politicians is typically the end of their elected period."
Roy Pederson

"As a politician, I view data as a drunk views a light post, not so much for illumination, but for support."
(Author unknown)

"Old established neighborhoods, *some as old as five years.*"
(Author unknown)

"The last principle I have to offer is a very simple one. Any program that is going to be successful will have to start with small things."
Bill Donaldson

The following are from the January 2020 issue of *New Mexico Marketplace* (NMM), again without my having requested permission; I prefer to see it as a quid pro quo, where NMM gets further publicity for their very fine local, monthly magazine.

"One should always play fairly when one has the winning cards."
Oscar Wilde

"Let no one ever come to you without leaving better and happier."
Mother Teresa

"If it weren't for Philo T. Farnsworth, inventor of television, we'd still be eating frozen radio dinners."
Johnny Carson

"The trouble with having an open mind, of course, is that people will insist on coming along and trying to put things in it."
Terry Pratchett

"Laughter is an instant vacation."
Milton Berle

Thoughts, Personal

(Hand Towel)

I Do Not Want To Die An Old Man!

I have a choice, I *can* die an old man, *or*, I can die a vibrant soul/heart/mind/body-of-someone-who-happened-to-be-born many years ago! (78 years in my case at this point; but it easily could be 28 years, 38 years, 48 years, 58 years, 68 years ago ... even 88 years!)

How long ago I was born matters little. Its only age-related significance is that I can no longer walk three miles a day as I did just a few years ago.

Just 10 minutes ago when I was walking outside, I caught myself starting to *waddle* side to side (as many do while walking at an advanced age). I decided to counsel myself to move forward with strides of a foot and a half, rather than the little steps I had permitted myself to get away with. (I was getting more miles going side to side than I was moving forward. If you cannot immediately picture what it is to walk "going side to side," just picture walking penguins.)

Update: On the last day of my 79th year, I walked three miles. On my 80th birthday, I also walked three miles ... and none of these miles were waddling.

Of significance is that now there are a few other things which I cannot do, for instance, dunk a basketball. (Truth: I never could dunk a basketball, although I did play center for about two weeks when I was in high school; proudly, I have several stitches on my scalp and a slightly broken nose from that experience.)

Nonetheless, there are several long lists of things that I still can do, many of them in very creative, mental *and* spiritual ways. I am proud to say that many of these are things I can do even better now than I did 20/30/40/50 years ago!

So, therefore, I must continue to inspire myself to live my life in such a way that I will die a vibrant soul/mind/heart/body, engaging all my faculties to assure that I am using all those *unused towels*.

What Would I Do If I Only Had One Year To Live?

One: First and foremost. Assure that I am not leaving any *unused towels*, aka God-loaned talents and skills unused!

Two: Remove all potentially embarrassing items and put them in a box marked: **"Destroy upon my death. Please honor my request for privacy. Get thee to the shredder and/or trash bin!"** (An example of an embarrassing item was a suicide note I found when helping a friend clean out her sister-in-law's papers after her death, the note being from the sister-in-law's husband letting her know that he was taking his life because of her.)

Three: Dispose of all miscellaneous items so that no one has to waste time going through all the miscellaneous stuff, like cards to/from dad/mom/old friends/photos of people who no one will recognize, e.g., keepsakes from conferences.

Four: Leave the house and garage free of clutter, including mementos and other items that were not important enough to keep in the house. (If you do not know of what I speak, you clearly have not had to clear out all the stuff from your "paw or maw." *Mama Mia*, what were they thinking when they chose *not* to throw away all that stuff?!)

Five: Leave clear information and instructions about everything, e.g., keys to the safety deposit boxes.

Six: Emphasize the compliments for all my loved ones, especially those who seldom hear compliments because they are focused on criticism.

Seven: Stop delaying/procrastinating.

Eight: Empty out my bucket list, including these wishes: a) I wish to paint! b) I wish to sketch! c) I wish to use our good stuff, e.g., the expensive pens, highball glasses, and champagne flutes. d) I also wish to use all the *boxed* items I have instead of continuing to save them "for a rainy day."

Talking With God

I talk with God a lot; some things are too personal to get into detail here, like when I am constipated ... at this point my wife is hollering, "TMI! TMI!"

One day I was talking with God and I asked Him why She talks so much with me, and God replied, *"I talk with everyone. You just listen better so you know I am talking with you. Many of those with whom I talk do not pay attention and so they are not aware that I am talking with them.*

Most of the time, you are a better listener; and by the way, you do realize that you are not the only one who talks with me when you are constipated ... but you are one of the few who talks with me when you are not constipated. Even though I am God, it is nice to be thanked for a good pooh."

There was more, but I was chastised, *"You have become a better listener recently; you were not very good a few years ago. When you* were preparing to take your life, you were not listening at all. You were mostly doing the talking, blaming me for your misdeeds. Do you remember that? You were so busy blaming me for what was going on that you were not even aware that during the entire time, I never left you. I was looking over your shoulder, with a tear in My eye, not only for your anger towards Me, but for My sorrow that you were hurting and that you would not include Me in a loving way to be with you."

There's Something Not Right About This

I grew up at a time when women were expected to be subservient to men. It did not seem right, but there were no real role model situations that challenged "this fact." One day, I don't recall how old I was, but I remember witnessing something that made me think "there's something not right about this."

We were at my parents' home having dinner and apparently we had company since we had added the middle extension to the dinner table in order to accommodate eight people. There was no separate dining room, just the old-fashioned kitchen complete with the kitchen table. In order to have it fit in the small space, the dining table was pushed up against the kitchen counter, right in front of the kitchen sink and the drawers that held the knives and forks.

After saying grace, my father who was seated at the head of the table (on the end that was backed up against the kitchen counter) began looking around. My mother, who was seated at the other end of the table, asked him what he needed. He said he didn't have a spoon. She immediately got up and came around the table to the kitchen counter, having to ask him to move his chair so that she could open the drawer right behind him in order to get him a spoon.

I thought to myself, dad could have just turned around and gotten the spoon himself. Yet, my mother had gotten up from the other side of the table to accommodate his need. And please be aware that my mother was no subservient female. (In her day a woman who was not married by her early 20s would have been considered an old maid. She was still single at the age of 29, not because she had no marriage proposals; there were three serious ones that I knew of. In addition to *stubbornly* remaining single, she was the one who pursued my dad who was nine years younger than she was.)

As I watched her take the spoon out of the drawer and hand it him, then walk back to her end of the table, I silently thought "There's something not right about this."

But then I slipped back into "the way things were." I never gave it much thought until many years later when I had my second major experience thinking "There's something not right about this."

At this time I had just taken over an office with several engineers and other professionals. One of the secretaries was in my office when we were interrupted by one of the other people in the office who popped his head into my office and addressed her with a matter-of-fact tone informing her that when she was through "in there," he and the others were out of coffee.

I recall asking, "So why doesn't someone make some coffee?" (The reaction from everyone was a puzzled look, including from the secretary; this was deemed normal since it was the secretary who was expected to drop everything and make coffee.)

I immediately walked out of my office and went over to the coffee pot and put up a sign saying, "The last person to take coffee such that there is not enough left for a full cup, please make a new pot."

The intent was clear! "From here on, do not expect the secretary to make the coffee."

I had not realized that this was happening since I was usually the first person in the office in the morning, and the first thing I did was put on a pot of coffee. Thereafter, there was always a full pot of coffee; I was not aware that it was the secretary who had been interrupted several times a day to make coffee for everyone else. Fortunately, I was not one to be challenged about this.

Sometime later, however, at another new office, I *was* challenged. This time the issue was about an even more repulsive "There's something not right about this."

Again, it happened to be an office of engineers and other professionals.

I noticed one Friday afternoon about 4:30, one of the engineers dropped off a large stack of papers on one of the secretary's desk with the rejoinder that he needed 10 copies by Monday morning at 8:30. (This was back before word processors were omnipresent; the basic typewriter was the only tool for typing reports. The old, handy Xerox machine was the only tool for efficiently making more than one copy.)

I noticed the look on the secretary's face; she was visibly upset but said nothing.

I asked her if that was an unusual request. She replied, "No, that is typical of him."

Again, my clear thought was "There's something not right about this."

As it was, he and the other engineers made three to five times more money than the secretary. Also, in those days, neither comp time nor overtime were the rule.

I asked her how much time was realistically needed in order to get the reports done. She told me that depended on how many re-edits were going to be needed. (This gift-to-the-world engineer also had the habit of insisting on making last minute changes.) I told her that on Monday I was going to institute a deadline for submitting materials to be finalized that was reasonable. Being an engineer myself, I fully understood the need for accuracy in any documents going out to any of our clients. It was therefore fundamental that sufficient time be allotted to produce an accurate documentation of the professional work conducted by all those involved in the production of any report.

She and I worked out something to get his report done by Monday morning.

On Monday morning at our weekly staff meeting, I advised everyone that although the clients' deadlines were obviously critical, so were internal deadlines for their submittal of the materials to be prepared for the client. This internal deadline focused on the time tables for those needing something typed and copies made of good enough quality "to go out the door," a deadline that assured the secretaries had sufficient time to get the materials properly prepared. I stressed that unless previous arrangements had been made between the secretary and the engineer, the new deadlines would be "xyz hours" *prior* to *going out the door, not* prior to arriving at the client's office.

Of course, it was not much longer after this that Mr. I'm-too-important-to-have-to-follow-the-rules did not believe me and submitted a report at about 4:00 pm on a Friday again.

When I heard about that, I told him that he would have to make arrangements with the client to submit the report at a later time since he was not providing the secretary sufficient time to get his reports properly prepared. He stuttered a bit until he remembered that he was not in charge. Red-faced, he took his papers and walked out the door.

On Saturday morning I went into the office to get caught up on my work, and lo and behold, who else was in the office but Mr. I'm-not-as-in-charge-as-I-thought-I-was along with his wife, both diligently working on his report. He was too embarrassed and/or angry to say anything to me, but his wife gave me a slight wink.

More About The Sixth Level

One idea that I had still makes me smile. (I mentioned some of this in the chapter, "Miracles.") This idea occurred when I was building a planter in our backyard.

First, I rummaged through the garage and scavenged every carpenter's level that I had inherited from my father. Four of the levels were the old two-foot wooden carpenter's levels with only one bubble; two of the levels were metal with three bubbles, one a two-footer and one an orange metal nine-incher.

My intention was to dig a solid trench in the caliche (a soil is that is as hard as cement) wide enough for the planter bricks which were four inches wide. In order to achieve a flat trough, I had to fidget with the levels in such a way that by aligning them end to end with some overlap, I could dig into the caliche maintaining the horizontal alignment around the curves all the time keeping one eye on the level bubbles. In order to maintain that horizontal plane, the bubbles all *had* to be near the middle of each level.

After an hour or so, I stopped to look at the six levels that I had spread out and saw that all the bubbles were *near* the middle meaning that the trench was close to being level.

At that time, however, I felt a tap on my shoulder.

As I steadied myself on the kneepad, I turned to look to see who was standing behind me, and seeing no one, I began to get up to *find* that person.

Before I could get up, I heard a voice ask, "What does water do?"

At first I said, "Huh? What do you mean?"

Then I realized that it must be Jesus who, even though He was an experienced carpenter, was just standing there, smiling at all my levels and thinking, "These humans – aren't they a kick! If they can make it complicated they will not hesitate to do so."

So as I pondered, "What does water do?" the answer was quite obvious: water flows downhill.

Therefore all I had to do was to scour the soil and pour water into the trench; if the water flowed in any direction, it meant that the trench was not yet horizontal.

When the water no longer flowed but rather *ponded*, it meant that the trench was flat, fully horizontal. My job was done!

My Baby's BD Today, Florence And Then On To Port Orford

We flew into Eugene, Oregon for Mary's special birthday.

[Years ago, we decided to live on a budget. It was a "let's keep track so we don't go crazy spending" budget, not a restriction budget. The Good Lord had given us the opportunity to work hard, make decent money *and* save frugally. We agreed that an important part of being frugal was to resist punishing ourselves; we therefore balanced our frugal spending with occasional "rewards." The larger reward budget items focused on taking a unique trip for each of our special birthdays ... birthdays ending in a five (5) or a zero (0).]

Mary had chosen as her special birthday trip a drive along the southern Oregon coast; hence the starting point was the airport in Eugene.

After picking up our rental car, it was only a 45-minute drive to the coast from the Eugene airport, a magnificent "Chamber of Commerce" type drive. It was so enjoyably charming that we did not mind the heavy RVs and large trucks pulling small and large boats, bumper to bumper, as part of the weekend traffic going to/from the coast.

We arrived at the River House Inn in Florence at four pm. Having researched details related to this trip, we had sought a room with the best views from the hotel; we asked for Room 108 overlooking the Siuslaw River.

After getting settled in, we drove next door to the Water Front Depot in Old Town Florence for dinner, again asking for a table overlooking the Siuslaw River.

Having studied the restaurant's menu before leaving Albuquerque, I knew that I had to have their clam chowder and their *arroz con mariscos* seafood plate. The menu listed it as *cioppino*, although it could also have passed as a version of *paella*, not quite either of them unless one is "a gringo" to true Italian or Spanish foods. No matter the correct name, it was absolutely the most delicious cioppino I'd *ever* eaten. (They called it "*arroz con mariscos* seafood bowl" ignoring the redundancy of "*mariscos*" and "seafood.") Mary had what she described as the best fish and chips she had ever had.

Since we fly into Eugene a few times a year to visit her mother, we agreed that on our next trip to visit Mom, we would fly in a few days early, not tell anyone and drive over to Florence, stay at the River House Inn, and enjoy dinner at the Water Front Depot. Mmmmmmmmm, *molto bene!* And *muy delisioso.*

After dinner, we returned to our room, moved the large dark blue sofa over to the floor-to-ceiling window overlooking the river.

We snuggled and enjoyed the river scenery.

As we sat there, pale-yellow and foggy-white street lights on the bridge over the river to our left slowly started to come to life, one by one.

Sea gulls and other birds continued to fly by, squawking and squealing to one another.

Across the river from our hotel, one light came on at a white, three-story house, replete with a wrap-around porch, outfitted with a white porch fence and lots of white porch furniture.

As we sat talking, gazing at the river traffic and occasionally looking over at the house, a second light came on upstairs. Soon, a downstairs light followed suit.

Mary channeled her childhood curiosity, wanting to know "Who lives there?" "What does the house look like inside?" "How many rooms are there?" "Whose room is it where the yellow-shaded lights first appeared?"

The childlike questions continued, "Are they having dinner in the downstairs?" "Why are they having dinner this late? This is Oregon after all – lots of old farts like us. They probably still eat 'supper' not 'dinner' although this *is* Sunday ... but Sunday dinner would more likely have been an early-midafternoon meal."

We laughed at her youthful curiosity. At that moment our ages were irrelevant; we were just two little kids asking silly questions *and* making up answers that made us giggle. ("I'll bet they're having fried chicken." "I hate the drumsticks." "I'll bet you the children are arguing that this is not supper, it's dinner!" "I'll bet you they are going to be eating a white coconut cake, with home-made vanilla ice cream with some of those Oregon black huckleberries.")

A few hours later, although this trip was my baby's special birthday trip wish, she was sound asleep after again describing the best fish and chips she had ever eaten in savory, enticing terms.

On the 17th, we left Florence in the late morning, arriving in Port Orford late afternoon. It rained all the way. In fact, it had drizzled an easy misty rain every day since we left Eugene on Sunday afternoon, all day on Monday, and all day Tuesday.

Nonetheless it was a beautiful drive in the rain. The traffic was not bad. All good highways.

We were staying three nights in an apartment loft, the Redfish Loft, one story above the classy Redfish Restaurant. When we got settled into the room, it was nearly dark outside due to the overcast skies. Although we could hear the ocean waves crashing on the rocks outside our room, all we could see were dark gray and black ominous clouds extending as far as the eye could see in the dim after-sunset light.

Tuesday being Mary's birthday, I had planned a special dinner at the Redfish Restaurant but just before we arrived, they decided to close the restaurant on Tuesdays. No matter, we decided to celebrate Mary's BD the next day, the 18th, even though that is the date of our wedding anniversary.

As a temporary option, we agreed to a mini-celebration of dinner at the laid-back eatery, The Crazy Norwegian, next door to the Redfish Loft where we were staying. The Crazy Norwegian was also a special place which we were eager to experience. (Please refer to the chapter, "Brief Encounters, Dianne in Port Orford.")

Although not the fancy dinner with appetizers, cocktails and a fancy dessert that I had planned for Mary's birthday, The Crazy Norwegian served us a scrumptious meal of fried oysters and "Po-girls" sandwiches.

This being Mary's birthday trip, when Dianne, the owner, came over and asked, "Is there anything else you would like?" I blurted out "Ice cream!" since I had promised Mary all the ice cream she wanted on this special trip.

When Dianne asked "How many scoops would you like?" Mary without blushing *declared*, "Four scoops!"

Dianne looked at her quizzically and then returned a few minutes later with a plate overflowing with *five* scoops of ice cream. Dianne had just made "a friend for life" with that gesture.

The next day, we enjoyed Mary's birthday, as well as, our 20th wedding anniversary at the Redfish Restaurant. Ice cream included!

Daddy's Little Girl

I hope my daughter is not embarrassed by what I am going to say: My Father's Days are made extra special by "Daddy's Little Girl" (DLG).

I am told that when our kids grow into adulthood, they are frequently embarrassed by having "dear old Dad" continue to refer to them by the nick-names they had when they were little girls or boys. In my case DLG passed her 50th birthday recently, a little into her adulthood one might say.

She may also be embarrassed that I often describe her one-hour-old, new-born baby face as "the face of a little mouse." (Come on, admit it, except for the mother who has labored for nine months to give birth to the little darling, most folks have not seen *a really* pretty baby. It's amazing what a few hours does for the little darlings' faces, turning them into gorgeous little angels.)

And just as "The Hungry Little Caterpillar" grew to be a beautiful butterfly, so did my DLG grow from her early-hours into a very beautiful young lady, and at age 50 is prettier than ever.

In the case of my DLG, her outward beauty is overshadowed by her inner beauty, which was fully displayed when she unselfishly moved 2,000 miles to take care of her Grandpa when he needed a 24/7 caregiver. As difficult as some of us get as we age (which Pop certainly *was* difficult), she continued to lovingly care for "the grandpa she held on a pedestal early in her life" until he took his last breath when he was 94 years old. (A few days before his death, he expressed some very sweet words about how much he appreciated her.)

Father's Days come and go, but "Daddy's Little Girl" makes sure that "Father's Day" pops in (cute, eh?) for an occasional visit throughout the year.

Regrets, I've Had A Few ...

In addition to the usual regrets, I have one special regret. While I was serving with the 4082 CMBT SPT GP (SAC) at Goose Air Base, Labrador as a 22 year old, I had the special pleasure of seeing the Aurora Borealis (aka the Northern Lights) on so many nights. Perhaps being so young, I did not fully appreciate what a spectacular view I was seeing.

After a few weeks, I recall being more interested in walking quickly from the "Goose Hilton" to the movie theater to see the latest Bond movie. The urgency of getting to the movie theater to catch "007" was that "connections from home" came infrequently; the planes from McGuire AFB carrying these connections including our mail came only when the weather permitted.

There I was, "live and in person," with the dancing lights of the Aurora Borealis just over my shoulder to the north, one of God's countless spectacular creations ... just taking it for granted; just like God's unconditional love, how many times have I taken that for granted?

There are so many other astonishing handiworks wrought by God, most of which we will not get to see, like the never-ending galaxies or the abundant, colorful life at the bottoms of our oceans. We will never know until we get to Heaven how many more spectacular creations God has produced, and is still putting together.

I regret not fully appreciating *the one* special creation of God that I did get to see.

One With The Horse

This "Personal Thought" goes full circle, from riding a beautiful black mare on a beach in Costa Rica to memorializing that ride with my "One With The Horse" painting in Cloudcroft, New Mexico.

The "Story" has four parts, beginning with 1) riding the horse; 2) eating at Rebecca's Restaurant; 3) taking a five-day art class; and 4) capturing the horse ride on canvas.

Part 1) My older daughter, Sash, included me in her and her husband's dream trip to Drake Bay on the Osa Peninsula in Costa Rica where they deep-sea dived and explored Cano Island, a unique biological reserve, for a glorious four days before we toured the rest of Costa Rica. Sash is a meticulous researcher and planner and found this first-class lodge, the Aguila de Osa Inn, which was accessible only by boat at that time.

Her loving reason for including me was that she was aware of my struggle with some suicidal issues. She also understood me well enough to know that I would not be a bothersome "third wheel." For instance, when she and her hubby went scuba diving, I busied myself with other activities.

One day for example, I and two other guests were escorted on a memorable horseback ride along the beach leading into the rainforest where we visited old abandoned native villages before returning to the beach.

This horseback ride has turned into a dream of a lifetime, which I have memorialized in a painting which I have named "One With The Horse."

As we emerged from the Costa Rican rainforest and back out to the two-mile long beach leading back to the lodge I, for some unexplainable reason, sensed that my horse, a large black mare, would like to get back to the stables where it was boarded ... without having to *slowly* and gently trot back.

Without thinking twice and with great confidence, I dropped the reins and let the horse go at its own pace.

She quickly got into a fast gallop as "We" raced back along the crescent-shaped, white sandy beach with the stables in view. The gentle ocean breeze caressed my face, reinforcing the confident knowledge that "the horse and I *were* one." Unbelievable!

She gradually slowed down when we got near the stables as though aware that "We" might not survive a sudden stop.

For those magical 15 minutes, I *was* "One With The Horse."

Thank you, Sash.

Part 2) Having dinner at Rebecca's Restaurant was a ten year venture.

Some years ago, my wife and I stayed in Alamogordo, New Mexico while conducting a workshop. For dinner we ventured the 20 miles to eat at Rebecca's, a very popular restaurant in the aptly named 7,000-foot elevation Village of Cloudcroft.

My wife enjoyed it so much that she asked me to take her back there again. Ten years later I did. (It took a while, but I fulfilled my promise.)

The reason that Rebecca's is relevant to this story is that we planned on staying a few nights at The Lodge where Rebecca's is located. I therefore had googled "What to do in Cloudcroft." It was then I discovered that art classes were a popular pass-time during the summers in Cloudcroft. After studying the various classes offered, I was inspired by the works of one of the guest artist teachers, David M. Kessler.

After googling his website, I was totally captivated by his abstract artwork as well as his dynamic style of painting.

And so, the two-night stay at The Lodge turned into a full week with opportunities to dine with "Rebecca" more than once. Mary liked that!

Rebecca, the "resident ghost," a stunning, young red-haired chamber maid who "walks the halls" of the Lodge and restaurant, even toyed with us during one meal. She was sweet about it.

Part 3) As I mentioned above, I signed up for David's five-day art class, a truly unique experience.

Besides David's fascinating style of acrylic abstract artistry, I was also entertained by the rest of the class, all women from Texas who traveled the several hundred miles to David's class. Fortunately, I had a Texas connection with them having been stationed at three Air Force Bases in Texas, Goodfellow in San Angelo, Sheppard in Wichita Falls, and of course, Lackland in San Antonio.

This art adventure was a fantastic way to revive a life-long suppressed desire to paint, one which I had put away during my college years due to a "I ain't good enough to even try" feeling.

David's humorous and energetic method of teaching would not entertain that sort of pessimism. I believe David does not even know that there is such a word as "pessimism." Thanks, David. You da Man!

Part 4) Evidence of learning that I *was* "good enough" to paint is my commemorating on canvas during David's art class that magical 15-minute ride on the sandy white beach in Costa Rica, letting go of the reins and trusting the dark black mare to share the adventure. The canvas, "One With The Horse," proudly hangs on my office wall and speaks gently to me every time I walk in and out of my office.

And this closes the circle.

TOSTI

(Bath Towel)

Introduction To TOSTI

This chapter is the main focus of this book. Simply, it *is* the fundamental reason why I have written this book.

It offers a look into a very lonely world where someone takes their own life while leaving no discernible clues that they were suicidally depressed ... leaving loved ones with unanswered questions.

Why didn't you tell me that you needed me? If you did tell me and I didn't understand, please forgive me.

I'm sorry that I wasn't there when you needed me most, but I really wonder, and would like to know ... would you have let me hug you and would you have let me into your world?

I wish I could go back to when we were together so that I could hold you tightly enough to show you that I truly cared about you.

Challenging as it may be, *I write this with the hope that these words be felt*, not just read. It is important to me to make an effort. *Even if this helps only one person*, I will deem it a worthwhile effort.

This chapter particularly addresses (a) those who have been left behind after a loved one "unexpectedly" takes their own life; (b) those who are currently overwhelmed with not knowing what to do for that loved one about whom they care and with whom they are currently struggling to connect; and (c) anyone who may be interested in thoughts based on my own experiences in that very lonely world.

I call that lonely world TOSTI; that is my acronym for "The Other Side of The Ice."

My first travel into TOSTI occurred back in 1993 when I considered submitting an article to *Parade Magazine*. The article was titled, "Thoughts In Preparation For Taking My Life."
(Please note: This was written 27 years ago.)

By the end of this month, I intend to take my life or in words which I prefer, 'to transition to another life.' Taking my life is not what I wish to do. It is the only action I feel I can control. Healing my hurts hasn't worked. Ceasing to be a disappointment to certain people who were very important in my life hasn't happened. Correcting my life seems impossible.

God and friends who care are not part of the world in which I exist. Sorry, dear friends. Sorry God.

The article ends with the following:

I have nothing else to add. Instead I cry every time I read my words.

I wish I were someone else so that I could hold me, love me, look into my eyes and feel my hurt.

Then, I believe I could love me and give me a reason to want to live and love.

It was at that time that I began to call the state of mind that I was in, "TOSTI."

(Note: Although this chapter is my main focus, it is rather *heavy* to absorb. This and three other chapters, "Suicide," "I'm Sorry Kids," and "Living In My Failures" contain difficult material. To provide a balance of lighter material, I have also included 19 other chapters that contain fun and uplifting "bits and pieces." Even as I was writing the earlier drafts, I found it necessary to take time out to read fun and uplifting words. If I did not take a break once in a while, I found myself overwhelmed with the memories of the journey through suicidal depression. *You may find some of this hard to read; I did.*)

What TOSTI Is

This discussion of TOSTI is not simple. I have struggled many hours to share what that experience is like. Describing what TOSTI embodies is extremely complex. Forgive me if I do not make it simple to understand; as I write this, I am very aware that I am sometimes rambling. However, my thoughts are written here not to win a grammar contest but to communicate sincere, deep feelings, not always expressed in straight-forward, rational thoughts and not always reflections that are gathered in complete sentences. My main purpose is to explain why some of us may be *out of reach* for you and your concerns for us.

I doubt that any of you have ever been aware of what TOSTI is, but I would not be surprised that you have been exposed to TOSTI.

Again, if you have ever cared for someone who *unexpectedly* took their own life and afterwards you felt disappointed or puzzled that they had been out of reach for you, and you had not been able to recognize the degree of their depressed state of mind, you *have* very likely been exposed to TOSTI. *The loved one who you could not reach was likely in the state of TOSTI.*

TOSTI is a state of belief that *nothing matters.* Love does not exist. Help does not exist. Caring does not exist. Feelings do not exist; even hurting does not exist. *None* of these exist on "The Other Side of The Ice." TOSTI is a total state of emptiness. Curiously, TOSTI is a *safe* place where nothing matters ... where one is in so deep that almost nothing can reach us.

Trust me, it is not about you; it is solely about the person who is on TOSTI. Wondering "Where were the clues?" would most often be a futile effort since there is a very high probability that *there were no obvious clues*. When fully on TOSTI, we have no emotions to share, whether positive or negative. As a result, "giving a clue" is really impossible. That is one of the reasons why a person on TOSTI avoids personal contact; *we have no emotions to share!*

During my TOSTI days, I had a friend who was the person who most often reached out to me. Every Thursday or Friday afternoon he would call me to encourage me to join him and our friends for drinks as we used to do.

His persistence in calling me, I believe, was because he sensed that the fun, engaging guy he had known me to be was dealing with some overwhelming issues. He knew for instance that I had been recently divorced. Unfortunately, my dear friend had neither the patience nor the insight on how to reach out to me in a manner that would have made me respond in a positive way.

His way of showing that he cared was to badger me with insults, often mixed with sarcasm, "What's the matter, did you get married ... again?"

While I *now* appreciate that he *was* trying in his own unique but unproductive way to show me that he cared, his way was not helpful and did not connect with me at the time. First, *they were just words*, something with which I had no emotional tie much less a tangible connection. *Actions, not words,* were what I needed to help me get out of my TOSTI world. As long as I was in my TOSTI state of mind, nothing anyone *said* mattered.

In a way that is difficult to explain, *discernible actions* would have gotten my attention while I was on TOSTI, and I would likely have begun to move out of that TOSTI world. Please understand that the TOSTI world is often a very temporary state of mind. While *moving out* of TOSTI is not easy, dropping back in to that state of mind can happen in a heartbeat. (If you have not experienced that lonely world of being in so deep that words do not matter, it may be difficult to understand this. I am confident however that any of my brothers and sisters who have been in a depressed state of mind this deep would understand what I am saying.)

Were I *not isolated* in my TOSTI world, I likely would have been open to feelings. I suppose what I would have wanted was for my friend to ring my door bell and say, "Get your coat, *and* be sure to bring your wallet; you're buying the first round." That action would have *showed* that he cared and I likely would have done what he said. Action!

Knowing my friend, he probably would have said something like, "You look like hell; I'll wait while you take a shower and shave. You got any beer?" As I coherently think back now, that likely *would have made* a connection with me. Again, not just words, but *words linked with action!*

I mention this to emphasize that actions, even if not the best offered, are a lot more valuable to someone on TOSTI. Essentially don't worry about whether your actions are or are not the best way to show that you care, even a "higgledy-piggledy" action will likely get a positive result. One seemingly small act could be a life-saver for the person on TOSTI. And please do not let your ego get in the way; we may not acknowledge that we felt your act of caring. *Show* that you care; it won't hurt and it just may help!

Unfortunately, I was not there for my friend when he took his life years later. I was upset with him for how he had treated his wife and his boys. I had not learned at that point what I learned from Rose from Port Orford, "It is not whether they *deserve* your love and caring ... but whether they *need* your love and caring." When he called me a few weeks before he took his life his chitchat was not replete with his usual sarcastic humor ... just a little scattered joking ... not typical of him ... *I should have known!* This was not my friend as I knew him to be; I should have sensed that this was his goodbye call. *I* should have gone to his door, rung his doorbell and gotten him out *to do something*. Instead, I let my ego get in the way and concluded that he did not *deserve* my caring. I regret that I was not the caring soul I should have been, one who recognized that he *needed* my caring.

Knowing what to do is not easy, especially if the first step is to get past questioning whether the person deserves our concern, versus whether the person *needs* our concern. If I care enough for the depressed person, I should offer *some* action.

When one is "above the ice," (in a "normal" state of mind), suicide may not make sense. But when we slip onto "The Other Side of The Ice," whatever sense there was "above the ice" is no longer relevant.

When on TOSTI, I could see and hear people who were "above the ice," but I was totally numbed by a barrier between what made sense and what did not. The result was that there was nothing to be gained from anything *being said* to me.

Often when people were just talking and I was not feeling any connection, my only solution was to retreat into my own safe world where I was relieved of emotions. If by chance, I was on the verge of actually feeling anything, I was also free to move deeper in my safe place. There, I could quietly sob to myself, or, sometimes, release a torrent of tears. Even if these tears lasted for hours, I strangely felt safe from disappointing others.

The saying that "words matter" is not relevant when dealing with someone who is on TOSTI. This is one time when *words do not matter. Only actions matter!*

A sincere hug did more for me than the words, "I care." (This is likely one of the reasons why dogs or cats speak louder than words with their wag of the tail, or their bringing you a gift of a dead mouse. ☺ These and the smile of a baby are more valuable than just words. Believe me those simple gestures are uplifting.)

Again, when dealing with someone on TOSTI, actions may reach the person, but words without actions have little chance of affecting the person.

Understanding TOSTI may help explain why you might not be able to help, why possibly no one can help. Even prayer does not help because on The Other Side of The Ice even God doesn't really make sense. If God does make sense, it is with a minor measure of "making sense," not sufficient to make the connection with life and love and caring, even a connection with a God whose love for us is unconditional. On TOSTI, God just does not exist to the point where "unconditional love" makes sense.

We *are down* and we are on the path to transitioning our lives out of this world. Our lives are *not* about staying alive; we've exhausted all the abilities we believe are at our disposal.

If our doors are closed for long periods of time, we are likely on TOSTI. If we don't answer the phone, if we don't want to go out like we used to, or, if our personalities change without explanation, there is a very good chance that we are on TOSTI.

My doors would be closed for days at a time. My telephone may as well have been "off the hook" during those times, since when it did ring, my reaction would be "that's not for me" even though I lived alone.

Life at the time was a series of the days being the same, one after the other, nothing different ... get up mid-morning, probably brush my teeth ... out of habit and for no other reason.

I might then go into the kitchen, scramble something to eat and drink. Then take it to the living room, lie down on the couch, turn on the TV, watch the OJ Simpson trial ... do anything that required neither thinking nor having to make decisions. On weekends I would just stay in bed or get up to go to the bathroom and then turn the TV on to whatever would just kill time and make the day go by faster ... or maybe go to bed earlier than usual ... then get up in the middle of the night and turn the TV on ... in and out of TOSTI.

During the week *or* the weekend ... it did not matter which – they were basically the same ... wearing the same pajamas for days at a time. Once in a while I might switch to shorts and a tee shirt when the pajamas got too stinky since I did not want to walk across the court yard to the laundry room because I did not want to have to talk to anyone, including people I did not know. I might have felt like I needed to shave.

In between, crying for no reason ... and not caring.

Whatever was happening, I made sure that I was never far away from "my safe place." I carried my safe place like a child carries his or her "blankey" except that it was something that no one else could see but which *I knew was there.*

It was nothing fancy, just a safe place into which I could quickly crawl into and zip up behind me. This even happened when I was alone in the apartment, but something on the television got my attention and not in a positive way. I would shrug and imagine, "Uggghh, I have to get out of here ... I need to get into my safe place bubble."

Once in a great while I would go to the mall, but I would do it during the mid-morning when I was not likely to run into anyone I knew. But just in case I ran into someone, I would walk next to the windows as though I were interested in the window displays ... always being sure not to have eye contact with anyone, whether I knew them or not ... not wanting any human contact. My being at the mall was not about being around people; I'm not sure what it was about.

Once in a while I would go to the movies, but I would assure that I got there *after* the lights had been turned off in the theater, *and* sit in the last row right by the door *and* be sure to get out of there before the lights went back on ... and for sure hightail it to the parking lot and leave quickly ... once in a while panicking if someone else was also leaving early, especially once when it was someone I knew. I heard them call my name but I pretended I didn't hear them and just kept going ... I had to go out of the parking lot a different way than how I drove in so that I would not have to drive by them.

Again, TOSTI is a state of mind and soul like no other; it is a journey like no other!

TOSTI is a condition that sometimes precedes suicide. However, understanding TOSTI does not presume to advise what to do with someone who is suicidal. It merely explains the state of mind and soul in which the person who is suicidal may be at the time.

For example, a form of TOSTI may be relevant to the state of mind of someone driving too fast and/or involved in a deadly single-auto accident. These are incidents that may portray "this does not make sense, but no one can make me see that it does not make sense, so just go away, get out of my way."

An article in the March 2009 issue of *Boomer* by Eric Billingsley, staff writer for the *Albuquerque Journal*, noted that "a study by the University of California at Davis Department of Psychiatry and Behavioral Sciences 'found that men's traditional views of masculinity and the stigma associated with mental illness lead to a tendency for them to reject a diagnosis of depression and to conceal or mask symptoms.' He quotes a Dr. Howard Ottenheimer, a clinical psychologist in Santa Fe: ' ... Many men have alexithymia, a condition where a person doesn't have the words to describe his or her emotions. When you ask how they're feeling, they say 'fine' ... They can't identify hurt, loneliness or fear ... '"

May I respectfully suggest two things: (1) they don't have the words to describe their emotions because they cannot *feel* any emotions; and therefore, (2) they cannot identify hurt, loneliness, fear, or any other emotion; when asked, "How do you feel?" ... the probable response for many of them could be "I'm empty."

(I do not want to get into a discussion that "we all have emotions." I know that we all harbor emotions, but one has to be able to "get them out" and "get in touch with them." Otherwise, it is more a matter of "I see you, but I cannot 'feel' you.")

Again, in that irrational world of TOSTI, love and caring do not exist. If somehow love or caring were present, it's likely present for only a short period. In that world of suicidal depression, love and caring are no longer experienced. This lack of feeling is probably "life-saving" ☺ since we will feel nothing. When you walk away, we'll not be disappointed.

While I was on TOSTI, business successes were non-existent in my mind. The fact that I had developed and presented very successful workshops when I was "above the ice" meant absolutely nothing to me when I slipped back to The Other Side of The Ice. In fact, having a successful workshop and feeling good about it often contributed to my "worst times" because I knew that feeling good would not last long ... some "bad" thing was likely going to come along and I'd be back in the TOSTI hole.

Our lives are *not* about staying alive; we've exhausted all the abilities we believe are at our disposal.

We spend an inordinate amount of time checking on what combination of pills will do the trick or we'll focus on the Sunday night movie when the doctor says to the victim's relatives, "She's all right. She didn't cut deep enough." We make a note: "I have to remember to cut deep enough."

There will be significant periods of time when we cannot talk to you due to our fear of breaking down crying. During these times, you're not likely to get us to answer the phone; we often have to wait until we're rational enough to return your call. It may be hours, it may be days before we can call you back. The longer we wait to call you back, the deeper we're likely hurting.

I know that when I went through my three years of suicidal depression, I could not, or would not, talk with anyone for days at a time. Friends who at first called me to go out for a drink eventually stopped calling me.

Those of us ready to transition, either seriously thinking about it or preparing for it with razor blade or pills in hand, often do not cry; we feel nothing, little or no love and therefore there is nothing to express. We *really* have nothing to say.

If we could believe that even one person truly loved us, we'd not want to transition. Believing that someone truly loves us has little to do with whether someone actually does love us. In my case, I'd rationalized everyone's "love" as being due to their being family, friends, or someone for whom I'd done something, or someone who had gotten used to my warts. There was only one person in my life who I believed did find me attractive since she hadn't had time to be aware of my failings; I'd done nothing for her before we met. One person in my life! And I have no idea where she is now. (Note: A reminder that this was written in 1993, three years before God sent me the four angels about whom I have written in this book, including my miracle of miracles, my wife.)

We don't believe you love us because we don't believe we deserve to be loved. It doesn't make sense "above the ice," but on The Other Side of The Ice, it makes sense! We need to re-learn how to accept love. In a way, we are back in the kindergarten of love.

It is complex and most likely not easy for you to understand. I don't understand it and I was living it. Don't feel bad should you not understand; it *is* quite complex, and TOSTI is comprised of things that you likely have never experienced or even been aware of. It *is* the other side of the ice.

I wrote then, "*I cry so much anymore that I don't bother wiping away the tears.*"

In our muddled little lives, we expect that things are going to go wrong. Things going wrong were my pattern of life for over 11 months. Whenever something appeared to be working out, something more horrid came along to knock me down ... real or imagined failures!

That had been my reality for such a long time that it became my pattern of life. Or at least that is what it seemed like on The Other Side of The Ice. Good stuff doesn't happen to the point where it is significant enough to be a part of our lives.

Many of us have been givers all of our lives. The result is that we do not know how to receive nor ask for help. To make it worse, most of you still want us to remain strong *for you.*

Others with sincere hearts are disappointed when they do something positive for us and we still don't come out of our depression.

We became depressed over many issues in our lives; you will not get us out by making us feel better over one issue that you feel comfortable talking with us about. Sorry, very sorry! It is not that simple.

Knowing that you love me is not enough. Love is as good in death as it is in life.

I can die happy knowing that you love me!

Why Understanding TOSTI May Help

A Few Personal TOSTI Experiences That May Help

As I said, this chapter is not about suggestions about what to do for someone who is suicidal. It is only about understanding TOSTI so that one is not surprised when a loved one "unexpectedly" takes their life. It is to understand TOSTI for those who may lament after someone has committed suicide, *"Why didn't he/she tell me?" "What was the clue that I missed?" "She/he seemed so happy; what went wrong?"*

There were many experiences with loved ones who reached out to me when I was on TOSTI. Some did their best; some unknowingly did their worst. Their actions reinforced for me that the safety of being on TOSTI was where I preferred to be. When on TOSTI, they could not hurt me ... I was shielded from anything they might say that would make things worse. *You can't hurt me when I am on my side of the ice.*

First, please understand that *sometimes* on TOSTI we may recognize warmth and love. We won't necessarily accept it, but we will be aware of it. A hand reaching out and touching us, an arm sincerely wrapped around our shoulders conveys "I care." We will not likely respond immediately but don't let your ego get in the way of sharing your love with us just because we're not responding. (If you can't handle this, then please just go away. We don't want your *conditional* concern.)

Assure that talking *to* us is not merely an exercise in ego satisfaction. Understand us. Don't try to cure us; help us care first. If nothing else, *show* that you care; don't just tell us that you care.

Dealing with us requires a lot of stamina and conviction. This is why we are disinclined to bother you. We did not get into this depth of depression in an hour. We're not going to get out of it with an hour of conversation with you. If an hour is all you have to offer, save yourself some stress. It won't do us any good and it may just upset you.

For me, one simple gesture that was very heartening came from a wonderful 20 minute telephone call from my soon-to-be divorced wife's 11-year old daughter who called from her biological father's out-of-state home to wish me a Happy Fathers' Day. Again, no questions, expectations or suggestions, just love. That she was out of state and called one day *after* Father's Day was not relevant. She showed up ... she "knocked on my door!"

So what else can one do? Pray.

Be very aware and understand that if you start to work with someone on TOSTI, you may have to be committed to be in it for the long haul. (I never said helping us would be easy; it is not. So maybe it is better that you just pray for us, and leave us alone!)

Don't feel bad if you decide you don't have it in you to help us out of our quagmire. Even though we might like someone to help us, we're still okay with where we're going. When on TOSTI, we understand death. We are no longer afraid of death. Death is something special. Death awaits us.

Offering to help, and then walking away for any reason hurts us even worse. We will not trust the next person who says they care. Our defenses go up twice as strong and twice as high!! We start to avoid you. The isolation protects us!!

We may forgive you, but we wish you had never said anything that made us aware that you "knew." That puts an extra burden on us to pretend to be happy the next time we talk with you. (I know it makes little or no sense to those of you who have not "been there," but trust me, those of us who have been hurt and struggled know the hurt you cause us.) Unfortunately, raised expectations are always another huge nail in our coffins! We were hurting before you stopped to talk with us; we'll be hurting worse long after you're gone.

A priest at the Franciscan Monastery in Phoenix, Arizona (back in the 1970s), said to a class that most important was to break the cycle of depression: going for a walk, dreaming about what is good in your life, exercising, doing anything that is significantly different from what you have been doing while in the state of depression, anything that changes your physical or spiritual state of mind. One of the premier motivational coaches of that decade, Anthony Robbins, talked about "changing one's state."

Both of these suggestions were all well and good *and relevant when* one is "above the ice." But when one is on TOSTI, they are not practical. Unfortunately, when in the state of TOSTI, no other state exists except for two states, the State of Numbness and the State of the Final Exit.

Another irrational action for many of us is what I did when preparing to end my life: I called my better friends and relatives and in my happiest voice talked for several minutes. I wanted them to remember me as "happy," not as "that loser who couldn't get his act together!" Sadly, it was all a lie!

We want our last contact with you to be a happy one. We don't want anyone to know how depressed we are and possibly have you suffer after we are gone, asking yourselves, *"What could I have done? What signals did I miss? How could I have helped him?"* Knowing that you might wrestle with these questions long after we're gone may make us feel worse and so we will be sure *not* to give you any clues that we intend to take our lives.

Other *nonsensical* thoughts include wondering, *"Maybe* God *is* dead."

> I want to believe that God is alive. But I have problems imagining a God who created the world "in seven days" and then spends the next gazillion, trillion years just sitting around watching us "do His will." It does not compute.

> Sadly without God, for us there is no hope, little to no feeling of being loved or being lovable, no caring about ourselves or others, and little to no hope of being saved.

Regrettably, if there is a God, many of us may even feel that God has abandoned us. During those times, it is a roller coaster of emotions, between praying to God for help to cussing God for "toying" with us – "Just end this, you $#!" is often the message to God rather than saying a respectful prayer asking for help. It seemed like ending my life would be a lot easier; end the roller-coaster! I foolishly thought that was something I could control.

Again, when I was fortunate enough to escape back "above the ice," what had happened on The Other Side of The Ice made no sense to me either. Understand that the hope, the love, the caring, the plans, salvation all occur "above the ice." When on TOSTI, there is no hope, no caring, no plans, no salvation.

This roller coaster with God manifested itself in dire ways. When I was "above the ice," there was a measure of happiness, but my greatest dread during this very terrifying time was the fear that sooner or later I was going to slip back to The Other Side of The Ice. Along with that happiness came the questions, *"How long is this going to last this time? What is going to happen that is going to drag me back this time?"*

At that time, God was not my salvation. In my mind, God was a big part of my problem; I blamed Him for everything that would not go the way I thought it should go. That is how irrational one gets when moving in and out of TOSTI.

Now 20 years later, I understand that God HAS ALWAYS BEEN here for me, watching silently over my shoulder, comforting me ... sad when I brushed away His loving hand.

When on The Other Side of The Ice, we often make foolish decisions. One morning, for instance, as I paid my monthly rent and saw that my checking account balance was down to "0," I realized that I would not be able to pay my rent next month. With a foolish sigh of relief, I took that as a sign that I should start my plans to "transition" before the end of the month. I began to prioritize what I needed to do, telling myself that "this time" I needed to finish the process. [Since I was giving myself a few weeks to "get this done," I may have subconsciously been allowing some time for someone to help me, even though I would likely refuse their help and fight them "to the death" resisting their offers. (Cute, huh!) However, I had never set a deadline before (no pun intended).]

At times like these, we just see no reason to keep on trying. We believe we've exhausted all "reasonable" options; none of them have worked. There may be reasonable options that *you* see, but there is nothing reasonable for us. For example, my sister's offer of financial assistance was two huge nails in my coffin for me. First, it reminded me what a sorry mess I'd made of my life, and worse, I knew that she recognized how messed up I was. Second, if I had accepted her loan, then I could not take my life until after I had repaid her. I was not willing to compromise my life/death for money! Ha! Really stupid eh? "Above the ice," yes really stupid; on TOSTI, it made perfect sense!

When I was suicidally depressed, the persons who hurt me the most were those who went through the motions of "caring about me." They would say, "Let me know if I can help you." My reaction was, "If you can't tell that I need you now, what makes you think you can help me later!?"

Well-meant but in the state of TOSTI, "offers" are not "lights at the end of the tunnel." To accept their offers would make me too embarrassed to share with them what a mess I was; I'd rather do the Final Exit with Thelma and Louise!

Don't *offer* to be there. *Be there!*

One of the four angels God sent me, Amy P., did not ask me if I were okay. Instead she respectfully was the adult; I certainly was not acting with my full capacities. She intuitively sensed that and so she said, "You're not okay are you." It was not a question but a statement made in no uncertain terms.

She followed that up with, "This is what I want you to do. Write down this number. Call when we hang up." She went on to explain who to ask for and what to say. Thank you Amy! *Words linked with action!* (Please see the chapter, "Angels We Have Heard On High, Angels We Have Felt On Earth" for more about my angel, Amy P.)

At one point, I learned that sometimes getting a depressed person to talk about anything gives them some respite from their self-afflictions. I used that intuition to help the 10-year old nephew of my bank manager, who had expressed concerns to me about her nephew constantly talking of committing suicide.

Pat (my bank manager), her nephew Ryan, and I met at a local park where we could be outside and still enjoy some privacy. He was an energetic little kid, who with some encouragement from his aunt, began to tell me why he talked a lot about suicide. (His reasons are not relevant here; what ensued from our talking is what is important.) Although we had little in common, he told me that part of his "depression" was that he had no one with whom to talk about things that he enjoyed without receiving some sort of judgment about what he was thinking. (His aunt not being aware of that often offered well-intentioned suggestions, which he took as a silent rejection of his feelings.)

And so Ryan and I talked about whatever he wanted to talk about. It worked. He enjoyed video games. He also liked to write but did not want anyone "criticizing the thoughts that he wrote down." From there we went to talking about other things that he enjoyed and again about the things that were bothering him. (Importantly, *he* took the lead. I was along as a companion.)

Surprisingly, he went back to talking about "writing." Now, I did offer a suggestion that was consistent with what he enjoyed. I told him that since I liked to write also, that maybe he and I could "write a short story together." He asked what I meant. I gave him an example where I would start the story; for instance, "Brian, maybe Ryan's age, was a writer. Not only was he nice and rich, he was also a very kind young man. One of his projects was to build a recreation hall for kids who had no money and could not afford to go to places that cost money. He called the hall, 'Brian's Home.' "

I told him that then he could write the next part of the story, send it to me and then I would add to whatever he had written.

We did this twice, and then his aunt told me he was writing "his own story." (He did not need me and my encouragement any longer.) With a big smile, I told her that was great. If he ever wanted to send it to me, to please tell him I would love to read it and that I wished him the best with that and the rest of his life.

Several months later, I moved out of town for a year, but before I left, I asked his aunt how he was doing. She gave me a hug and said, "He is a typical pre-teen now. Full of curiosity and dreams."

He/we had developed an actionable plan, with specific steps to be able to enjoy and appreciate the happy parts of his life. *Words linked with action!* That got him on the right path! (Not that it is particularly significant, but to further explain that he and I had little in common when we began to talk, not only was he 10 years old, but he was also blessed with a GGT (God-Given Tan).

A Few More Thoughts About Why Understanding TOSTI May Help

Remember that for a person on TOSTI, words do not matter; only actions matter. In whatever manner that works for you, *show* that you care. *Show* that they are not alone, and without preaching remind them that in addition to you, God is looking over their shoulders with unconditional love, patiently waiting for them to accept God's love.

Although I've said that this chapter is not about suggestions about what to do for someone on TOSTI, there are a few things that I feel strongly to pass on regarding *what not to do*:

Do *not* offer suggestions about how they can pull themselves out of their misery.

Do *not* ask questions that can be answered with "yes" or "no" answers. Find out what they are thinking that they *are* willing to talk about.

Do *not* ask, "Is there something I can do for you?" I *repeat*: do not ask "Is there something I can do for you?"

Do *not* say, "Tell me what I can do for you". (We will not tell you what we need. We won't, period. "No, thank you.")

Do *not* tell us to "just snap out of it!" If you do, please be aware that our only thought of you at that moment will be, "You are a real idiot, a complete, uncaring, "xy!/z*!~y" nitwit!"

Do *not* make a spectacle of praying for us. Silent prayers are more sincere since we know you aren't doing it for show!

Do *not* suffocate us with your "caring." A crushing hug or insincere smile communicates that you don't know what to say or do, so you are going to hold on to us and hope that we will tell you what to do or say. (Believe me; you won't like it if we do tell you what to do!)

Do *not* go through the motions of caring, and then walk away leaving us in an even deeper state of depression.

Additional Thoughts If The Loved One About Whom You Care Is A Teenager:

When teenagers lock themselves in a room for endless hours, they may be on TOSTI. In that case, invite them to do something with you that they will be interested in doing. It is important that what is being proposed is something that the young person has shown to be enjoyable or important to them. Say it with jovial confidence, not with a sad tone, or in a disappointed manner. Offer to do something which you know they enjoy doing and do it in such a way that you will enjoy it yourself.

Be with them for their benefit, not to make yourself feel better. Let them know that their thoughts and questions are important, that their reasons for doing things and not doing things are important. They need to know that they are special!

And if you are the teenager locked in your room, be self-confident enough to step outside and say, "Let's do xyz." Respectfully, do not accept a negative reply if you are on your way to TOSTI. Convince them to do something that you will appreciate. If they are not "being the adult," *you* "be the adult." You very possibly are the one with *the answer* about what to do to get you out of TOSTI. Do it!

Lastly, my caring encouragements for anyone stuck on TOSTI:

Escape from TOSTI *is* possible; I escaped from TOSTI and I know you will too. Ask for God's hand to help lift you out of TOSTI.

There is yet work to be done and *it can only be done by you.* Believe in yourself! Take a little time ... start with a small prayer and when you are able to acknowledge all that is good about you, create in your mind who you would like to be. Then, get to work with the next steps into becoming the person who will take God's hand and be guided to be the really good, smart, loving and loveable person who *you* can love!

God's hand is what did it for me. God can do it for you! Close your eyes if need be, and reach out ... take God's hand and don't let go!

God bless you.

Note: I've added the following just before this is going into the final printing step.

It is a tribute to Major General Mark Graham, USA (Ret.), Mrs. Carol Graham and their two sons, 2LT Jeff Graham and Senior Cadet Kevin Graham. Jeff was killed in Iraq and Kevin "lost his battle with depression."

They described their pride for their sons at the 2022 National Memorial Day Concert in Washington D.C.

Of Kevin, they shared, "We knew he was sad but we didn't know you could die from being too sad."

"We know there a lot of Kevins suffering in silence."

About The Author

Fil A. Chavez is the author of *Unused Towels*, a collection of refreshingly honest, real-life stories based on his lengthy, successful professional career in management and consulting as well as a fabulously rewarding personal life. He began writing while in college but the "writing bug" really bit him when he won an exclusive weekend at the superbly élite L'Auberge de Sedona, a luxury resort in Sedona, Arizona, for his "First Place" winning short story in a Romantic Essay Contest.

The chronicles shared in *Unused Towels* describe inspiring, thought-provoking incidents in the author's life ... some will bring laughter, some will evoke tears, some will elicit deep thinking ... some will require no thinking.☺

Some of the narratives in this book touch on deeply serious topics since one focus of the book is to shed light on suicidal depression. The author offers encouraging thoughts from his own personal experiences with suicidal depression, especially to those who have lost a loved one to suicide and wonder, "Did I miss the clues?" "How could I have not known?"

Importantly, many of the stories are humorous. All of them are uplifting and emphasize how great and loving God is.

He credits his wife, Mary, with lovingly encouraging him to continue to write the book. Important to him were comments she offered after reading early drafts of his book, like, "This is very funny!" and "I'm glad that God saved you for me."

He adds that he was inspired to finish writing the book by a nurse, Stephanie, who he met "by God's will" when they were in line for their first Covid-19 vaccination. "Your writing style allows the reader to truly feel like they are on this journey, meeting these 'characters' with you and Mary. Reading about your encounters is refreshing and reminds us how powerful simple conversations with strangers can be. I think the concept of this book is delightful and will entertain all types of people."

The book costs $9.18 in honor of Fil and Mary's *miracle* wedding date on September 18th. He describes this experience in the chapter, "Miracles."

Made in the USA
Middletown, DE
29 December 2022

18466839R10175